The Paper Bag Principle

The Paper Bag Principle

Class, Colorism, and Rumor and the Case
of Black Washington, D.C.

Audrey Elisa Kerr

The University of Tennessee Press/Knoxville

Library of Congress Cataloging-in-Publication Data

Kerr, Audrey Elisa, 1969-
The paper bag principle : class, colorism, and rumor and the case of
Black Washington, D.C. / Audrey Elisa Kerr.— 1st edition.
p. cm.
Includes bibliographical references and index.
ISBN 978-1-62190-265-2
1. African Americans—Color—Social aspects—Washington (D.C.)
2. African Americans—Race identity—Washington (D.C.)
3. African Americans—Washington (D.C.)—Social conditions.
4. Race discrimination—Washington (D.C.)
5. Washington (D.C.)—Race relations.
6. Washington (D.C.)—Social conditions.
I. Title.

E185.93.D6K47 2006
305.896'0730753—dc22
2006000655

To my family:
Neville and Mary Kerr
and Jennifer Arlene Kerr-Logan

Contents

Illustrations

Acknowledgments

When this manuscript was a dissertation, it was my pleasure and good fortune to have Dr. Barry Lee Pearson stand behind my work. His own commitment to African American folklore and oral history has been a flawless model to follow. For the financial support of this project, my sincerest thanks to Dr. Cordell Black, Office of the Vice President, University of Maryland, College Park; the Committee on Africa in the Americas at the University of Maryland; the Department of Graduate English Language and Literature, University of Maryland, College Park; the Simon's Rock College Faculty Development Fund; and, at Southern Connecticut State University, the English Department, Office of the Dean of Arts and Sciences (Dr. Donna Jean Fredeen), and the Minority Recruitment Committee.

For research assistance, I am grateful to the Moorland-Spingarn Research Center at Howard University, especially the very capable staff of the Manuscript Division. I would also like to thank the librarians and archivists at the Schomburg Center for Research in Black Culture; Xavier University Archives; the Library of Congress; Martin Luther King Library, Washingtoniana Room; and the Smithsonian Institution, American History Archives.

My deepest appreciation to Dr. Gladys Marie Fry for the direction that she provided throughout the many stages of this project. I also wish to thank the following people: Frank Harris, Dr. Marilee Lindemann, Dr. Verlyn Fleiger, Dr. Nicole King, and Dr. Alfred Moss, my readers; and Dr. Nancy Bonvillain and Dr. Kenneth Goings, who also offered helpful feedback. As always, I thank my dear friends Stacy Richardson, Michele Tiller, Angel Feemster, and Dr. Shelly O'Foran for their support. Finally, I am grateful

Acknowledgments

for the human insight I gain from Rev. John T. Meehan and my god-children: Justin Christopher, Sydney Kristen, and Cameron Alexis.

Also, I wish to thank the very capable staff at the University of Tennessee Press, especially my editors: Scot Danforth, acquisitions editor, and Gene Adair, manuscript editor.

This project began some ten years ago as a five-page paper in an under-graduate folklore class; it was the interest of my professor that gave it life. If this project is thought to be a useful contribution to the field of folk study, it is owed to the late Professor Gerald Davis, whose wisdom, manner, and commitment to "the word" precipitated my decision to study folklore and to whose life I pay tribute through the maturation of this work.

Introduction

In 1993 I met a young lawyer who attended Howard University Law School in the mid-1980s. We were both attending an annual fundraising event in Washington, D.C., called "Cartoons and Cocktails," and over drinks, she told me about a group of Howard Law School classmates she called "the beautiful people." These classmates, mostly native Washingtonians, had organized an on-campus, invitation-only graduation party, which they called a "paper bag party," an affair that was limited to their circle of friends. Most of the people in their circle were fair in complexion; the naming of the party thus signified to fellow Howard students that the gathering was limited to a handpicked, pre-identified, exclusive (and, more important, exclusionary) group, all of whom could be identified by their complexions, which were lighter than the color of a standard brown paper bag.

At the time that the Howard University Law School graduate told me this story, I was the managing editor of a news service for young writers in Washington, D.C., the same organization that was hosting the cocktail fundraiser. I was also doing graduate work in African American folklore. As an undergraduate, I had been lured into folk studies by an African American folklorist by the name of Gerald Davis, who believed that there was still much terrain to be mined in the world of contemporary urban African American folklore. At the time that I met Professor Davis, I was also pledging a black sorority at Rutgers University, and he utilized this scenario to convince me to complete a project on black fraternity and sorority chants—specifically, to consider the power that these chants have in shaping black community culture on a predominantly white college campus.

My interest in this material intensified as I thought about the ways in which this material was gendered, such that it created a very narrow parameter within which black women thought about beauty. "Beauty," so far as I could see, was still defined in traditionally European terms, with long flowing hair, lighter skin, and thin, lean builds signifying true beauty. Over time, my interest evolved into a desire to record the folk forms that African Americans used to discuss European concepts of beauty, including rhymes, chants, rituals, myths, and legends. Over time, and through many interviews, I also learned about the many ways that black women were challenging these traditional notions.

My chance encounter with the Howard University Law School graduate was instructive in three ways: First, it led me to consider that complexion folklore (including myths, legends, rumors, tall tales, folk beliefs, rituals and practices, and traditions) formed a body of material—though not identified as such—that held significant weight in black communities, both socially and behaviorally. Second, it confirmed in my mind that such folklore still maintained currency in black communities because racism still governed our cultural preoccupation with proximity to whiteness. And third, it demonstrated that while most black people knew about complexion lore, it had not been fashioned into a single, academically accessible body of recorded material; in other words, the stories were well known but seldom committed to paper.

The purpose of this book is to record lore in black communities about complexion, phenotype, and hair texture and to use this lore to explore the relationship between racial prejudice and interracial discrimination. I use the term "lore" to indicate that the material included here represents legends, rumors, contemporary legends, and—in the first two chapters—myths, rituals, proverbs, and community traditions as well. Patricia Turner uses the term "rumor" to refer to short-lived beliefs; "legend" to refer to "traditionally grounded" narratives of belief; and "contemporary legend" to refer to beliefs that also include modern motifs.[1] While I embrace and adopt these distinctions, this project also draws heavily from historical sources, including archival records, popular news sources, and advertisements; therefore, I would define this work as a cultural study with attention to folklore.

There are many contemporary and historical studies dedicated to recording African American lore; similarly, there are innumerable contemporary social studies dealing with the significance of complexion and class in black communities. Yet, there has not been a complete collection that documents the existence of this lore, places it within the larger tradition of African American storytelling, and links some of the subject matter of African American storytelling to the conditions that result from racism in America.

Thus, the objective of this study became threefold: to record lore related to the "paper bag principle" (the principle that granted blacks with light skin higher status in black communities), using Washington, D.C., as a representative model; to investigate the impact that this "principle" has had on the development of black community consciousness; and to link this material to power that results from proximity to whiteness.

This preoccupation with complexion, this residue of racism, race consciousness, and racial judgement, exists in every nation that has been influenced by Western world ideology. To this day, for example, India's version of Hollywood, Bollywood, is dominated by fair-skinned movie stars with European features despite the reality that most Indians have darker skin. In Brazil, the vast majority of the students at major universities are white in appearance despite the reality that most of Brazil's population bears physical evidence of African descent. Proximity to whiteness is still a passport to access and opportunity. Black America's telling of this legacy manifests itself, in part, in the form of paper bag lore.

Meaning of the Paper Bag Principle

I would categorize the material I have collected as urban folklore for two reasons. First, it emerges primarily in city centers where African Americans with some level of social leverage form groups that perpetuate an internal dialogue about color privilege while members of neighboring black communities or groups begin an external dialogue about the inner workings of the exclusive groups. Second, the fact that most black people have some familiarity with these stories—while most white people do not—also marks this material as urban folklore: the reach of these carefully protected complexion tales begins and ends in the communities of origin, and the tales bear witness to the problems that result from the aspiration to an outside standard, namely whiteness.

The Paper Bag Principle was chosen as the title of this book after long consideration and, admittedly, years of deliberation. Many African Americans will immediately understand my hesitation. The "paper bag"—the same object that is commonly recognized as the container of school lunches and supermarket groceries—becomes, through this lore, an object of complex, perplexing, and obscure meaning in black communities. The paper bag is both a source of pride and an objectionable taboo; it elicits a contagious curiosity because its color is the marker that distinguishes "light skin" from "dark skin" and it is believed, lore suggests, to "center" blackness on a continuum that stretches infinitely from literal black to literal white. Even more, in what is probably the most widely circulated and popular African American lore, the brown paper bag is believed to signify acceptance and inclusion (if one is lighter than the brown bag), as well as absolute rejection reminiscent of Jim Crowism. The title *The Paper Bag Principle* speaks to the power of lore in intersecting social, religious, and institutional norms. Thus, this study adapts an existing symbol of expression to examine a persistent intraracial social belief that has been sustained by all kinds of black American communities and circles for many generations.

Even given its derogatory meaning, the phrase "paper bag test" or "brown paper bag test" is traditionally used by African Americans in a variety of settings and with great frequency. Throughout the twentieth century, references to paper bag parties (gatherings for lighter-skinned blacks), paper bag churches (those catering to a fair-hued congregation), brown bag clubs, or brown bag social circles have resulted in a proscribed language of exclusion and exclusiveness.

This project should be read as an interdisciplinary study, drawing from sociology, history, and literature, and framed around complexion-related caste legends and rumors. Historically, black literary works have addressed color consciousness, from the first black American novel, William Wells Brown's *Clotel* (1853); to Frances Harper's *Iola Leroy* (1893), with its refined mulatto heroine; to Wallace Thurman's 1929 novel about "too dark Emma Lou" titled *The Blacker the Berry;* to Shirlee Taylor Haizlip's chronicle of color-struck Washington, *The Sweeter the Juice* (1994); to Marita Golden's *Don't Play in the Sun* (2004), which captures painful complexion rituals in a contemporary context.

Historians such as Willard Gatewood have argued that white standards of behavior influenced the culture and style of living of the black elite, who were "small in number and light in complexion," thus, quite literally, resembling the "better class of whites."[2] Similarly, Lawrence Otis Graham's *Our Kind of People* (1999) exposed the extent to which black aristocratic attention to complexion is, at best, a dangerous flirtation with white aristocracy and, at worst, a debilitating mimicry of it.[3]

Popular media, especially television, have also reflected the problem of color in an intraracial context. In the short-lived television show *Frank's Place,* the title character, portrayed by actor Tim Reid, is invited to become a member of the most restrictive black lodge in New Orleans, renowned for its exclusion of darker-skinned African Americans. One of Frank's employees holds a paper bag to her arm while informing him that because her skin is darker than the color of the brown bag, "her kind" would not be welcomed at the club. She describes "her kind" as darker African Americans—creoles with "a lowercase c"—and "their kind" as fair-skinned African Americans, Creoles with "an uppercase C." Frank decides not to join the club because he realizes that it perpetuates the same ill treatment of blacks as white social clubs. The same theme was introduced a few years earlier in the equally short-lived situation comedy *Sinbad:* the main character deliberates as to whether he will accept membership into an exclusive family-membership club (the club is fictional but is reminiscent of Jack and Jill of America, Inc., a black family organization) after he is told that the club once used a paper bag to keep out dark-skinned African Americans.

Methodology

Although this book began my efforts to record this lore, my awareness of it began in my home. I am a first-generation African American who grew up in a black West Indian household in New York. My grandmother, like many people of her generation, referred to black people as "colored." She was a very fair-colored woman who came to this country in her twenties, and after growing up in a black country, she immediately recognized the significance of color in American black communities. Moreover, she recognized complexion as the passport to better jobs and better opportunities in white communities. She had an easy time finding work, and, no doubt, her physical appearance was a valuable asset. It was an added advantage that she came from a family that was considered upper class by her small rural community's standard; thus she was both fair-skinned and moderately "polished." I learned the lesson early, and well, that complexion mattered, internally and externally, and in my small mental sky, this project was probably already taking shape.

The interviews for this study were conducted between September 1996 and August 1997 and in July 1999. Most of the interviews were conducted while I was a graduate student at the University of Maryland, College Park, living in a suburb of Washington, D.C. During this time, I was working in the District as a freelance news reporter. I was also an active supporter of the arts in the District, and these activities, along with my research at Howard University and at the Library of Congress, accounted for countless hours spent in the city. My interviewees were questioned about their educational background, occupation, and organizational and religious affiliations. They were also asked specific questions to determine their level of familiarity with complexion lore and complexion-related rumors and legends. A very small number of informants were not familiar with complexion test lore, but because their interviews shed light on the social mores of black Washington, they were included. Awareness of paper bag test lore, therefore, was not the only criterion for inclusion in this study: rather, interviewees were also expected to have lived in the District over a period of time and to have some awareness of the institutions, neighborhoods, and organizations that converge to form black Washington's cultural landscape.

In the course of conducting this study, I came to regard "truth" as a relative state that could not determine the value of this study. For example, I determined that, whether or not the practices discussed here could be proven, they were nevertheless significant in the development of racial and intraracial systems in the city.

I have included a disproportionately large number of informants from Howard University because Howard is not only the most historically significant institution in the city's black life but it has also been a consistent repository of stories about complexion. It was while using the archives at Howard that I identified the focus of this project and met many of the people who would become contributors to my research. My success rate through random meetings was probably greater (and certainly more diverse) than any formal network.

In the end, I selected the informants who (1) directly addressed the rumors and legends; (2) commented on the impact that tests had on their belief systems or behaviors; and (3) had a long enough history in the city that they could, to their own satisfaction and mine, reflect on the impact of stories and lore on black Washingtonians over time. The voices of interviewees other than these appear less frequently and with much less emphasis.

Some interviewees were Washingtonians with longstanding lineages in the city, but others were transposed into the District—these days, this is more and more frequently the case. All of the Washingtonians, however, were a cross-section of the following: (1) self-identifying African Americans; (2) Howard alumni and/or faculty; (3) religious leaders and District church congregation members; and (4) graduates of Dunbar High School or Armstrong High School (the two high schools traditionally serving black students in the District).

The interviewees were interviewed by telephone or in person. Some, according to their wishes, remain wholly anonymous in these pages. In other cases, I have used only first names and minimal identifiers such as present occupation and/or the year the interviewee graduated from college. On the whole, I found, to no great surprise, that the interviews conducted in person were more complete, more detailed, and, generally, more interesting. In a few cases I followed up phone interviews with a meeting. It was during the in-person meetings that I received the richest material. Sadly, some informants shared very personal complexion-related stories which they later decided to withdraw from their transcripts. In such cases, I have honored interviewees' wishes.

The completion of this book required great attention to the nomenclature used to write about and talk about hue. The language of complexion, like the language used to talk about race, is varied but highly specified. And, as Randall Kennedy notes in his book *Nigger: The Strange Career of a Troublesome Word,* "to be ignorant of [a word's] meaning and effects is to make oneself vulnerable to all manner of perils, including the loss of a job, a reputation, a friend, even one's life."[4] He makes this assertion with regard to the use of the "n-word" and indicates that, in his own childhood experience, the word "nigger" was part of a "widespread feature of African American culture that has given rise to a distinctive corpus of racial abasement typified by admonishment, epigraphs, and doggerel such as . . . 'If you're white, you're right, / If you're yellow, you're mellow, / If you're brown, stick around, / If you're black, step back.'"[5] I would argue that the brown bag principle is similarly inflammatory, for to indicate that one does not "pass" the brown bag test functions as a form of slur. The demonization of dark skin within African American folk forms is a charged and threatening act; it is an internal dialogue about race, racism, and racial stereotypes that turns such discussion into an intraracial negotiation.

As an example of highly specified nomenclature, the word "mulatto" is used sparingly and mostly in historical context. The word "biracial"—which also denotes mixed heritage but bears fewer historical burdens—is used with greater frequency. Neither term accurately addresses the condition of hue—that is, how much more complicated complexion is than ethnicity or race.

The terms "light-skinned" and "fair-hued" are used to describe people who self-identify as black but whose lighter coloring shows the predominance of, or evidence of, other heritages. "Racial ambiguity," then, is reserved for those whose racial identity is indistinguishable as black or white and/or those whose racial heritage is unknown. In the context of black life and in the larger context of America, the indistinguishable are banished, as it were, to the category of "people of color" and are thus limited in the access to opportunity that is implied by the designation "white." Thus, the category we might call "non-white" is nebulous and infinitely broad. I wish only to admit here that I am fully aware of the complicated meanings—the inferences and implications—that are drawn by the use of these terms and that they are given the task of accommodating historical anxieties that cannot easily be resolved. Rather than contribute to the subjective and divisive function of many complexion descriptors, I wish to state here that this language is, for me, an affirmation of the physical fluidity of race and a painful reminder of the detective-like, rigorous efforts of many to draw unmovable racial lines. This study does not suggest a new nomenclature to talk about hue. I have, however, tested and, I hope, exhausted the limits of the traditional vernacular, so far as the study of lore is concerned.

My greatest research advantages would appear to be superficial in most other contexts. They are my own complexion, which is neither dark nor light; my hair texture, which is neither terrifically straight nor kinky; and my features, which fall somewhere in the middle of the phenotype spectrum. I am not mistakable as anything but black, so it was my sense that darker informants identified with me. At the same time, this project was not exactly hindered by the fact that my coloring, as my mentor Gladys Marie Fry noted, is "you know, 'pretty brown.'"

I hoped to reach a point in my research when I felt that my interviewing was done, or that I had exhausted most angles of looking at complexion lore. Now, on the contrary, I have come to feel that the present voices raise questions that are left unanswered; in actuality, the range of avenues that complexion lore may take creates the necessity for many subsequent studies. It is my sincerest wish to represent the interviewees and their lore candidly. To this end, the stories here are taken from the mouths of District residents without the application of artistic license.

Chapter 1 of this book surveys the most poignant illustrations of complexion lore in American literature, African American folklore, and literary folklore generally. I am concerned, in this chapter, with the historical activity of complexion-related stories in the form of folktales, proverbs, rhymes and folk poetry, and ritual, as well as novels and novellas by black writers. While works of literature, anthropology, and history have dealt richly with complexion dilemmas, the folkloric example demonstrates how essential folklore is as a tool in understanding traditions—past and present—as they relate to complexion.

Chapter 2 begins with legends from American cities other than Washington. It offers a national perspective that helps frame a more focused consideration of lore in Washington.

Chapter 3 considers the settlement patterns among African Americans in the city. It includes a discussion of how intraracial separation among black Washingtonians was reflected in education, profession, wealth, and, consequently, social grouping. As an extension of this, chapter 4 surveys social and organizational patterns among African American residents in the District to consider the circulation of complexion legends along the social landscape of the city.

Chapter 5 focuses on complexion legends and rumors in two centers of black learning—Howard University and Dunbar High School. Howard represents a microcosm of Washington, D.C., in the same way that Dunbar is a microcosm of Howard University. Dunbar is included in this study to demonstrate both the range and diversity of rumors associated with the black academy; it will clarify how these stories were circulated among young adults.

Chapter 6 addresses the specific role of the black church in intraracial lore because, as the second-most powerful institution in black life, preceded only by the black family, the attitudes and choices of black churches reflect the attitudes and ideas of black communities. The two congregations receiving primary attention, the Fifteenth Street Presbyterian Church and the Nineteenth Street Baptist Church, were mentioned most frequently by informants when they discussed rumors of intraracial storytelling patterns in religious communities.

Chapter 7, the conclusion, reemphasizes the role of folk forms in recovering a city's cultural story. Moreover, it presents a contemporary perspective on traditional legends and discusses the ongoing impact of such legends on African American life.

About half of this project is the result of fieldwork. I also depend on photographs to produce compelling evidence of the traditions in which this lore is grounded. No amount of research or oral testimony can illustrate this as strongly as the visual images.

If successful, this project will offer an alternative social history of black community by highlighting beliefs about divisions in education, religious practice, and social organization based on complexion. It will also demonstrate the usefulness of folklore in recording traditions, beliefs, and customs of the black community in a way that centers such lore—which is generally amorphous and peripherally historical—in conversations about racial issues. This project, ultimately, uses one city to argue that complexion issues are more far-reaching and long-standing than most other intracultural dilemmas.

Chapter 1

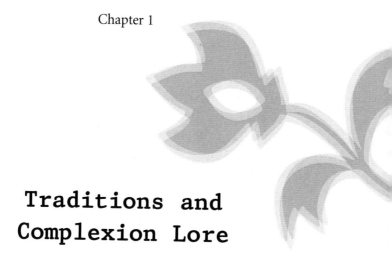

Traditions and
Complexion Lore

The problem of negative associations with blackness goes
deeper than aesthetics. "Black is evil!" was a retort intended
to account for behavior one disapproved of. . . . Everywhere
black people were pitied, for deep in the soul of even the
whitest Negro was an erosive self-pity that gnawed at his
vitals. The crucial question has always been a question of
identity: Who is this Negro whose identifying characteristic
is his color and what is his status in the world?

John Hope Franklin
Color and Race

In the 1929 Broadway production of *Hot Chocolates,* in Fats Waller's now-infamous blues song "Black and Blue," a black woman laments her dark skin and the burden it has become in an American social climate where privilege requires fair skin. "What did I do," she ponders sorrowfully, "to be so black . . . and blue?" The popularity of these lyrics by Andy Razaf, the reissuing of the song by several famous African American artists, the success of the play, and the incorporation of the song into the American blues canon all speak to the internalization of racialized speech in African American expressions. Faded black and white film footage of "Black and Blue" features a young Fats Waller surrounded by very fair black women, gingerly empathizing with the problem of "blackness" and subsequently "blueness." In one scene a fair black woman stands at the front door of what may be a Harlem rent party, inspecting all of the guests as they enter the affair. While all of the male visitors are medium or dark brown in hue, the female invitees are all light-complexioned. The lyrics state,

> Browns and yellers all have fellers
> Gentlemen prefer them light,
> Wish I could fade, can't make the grade,
> Nothin' but dark days in sight.[1]

This brand of music memorialized ideas of race, color, and caste, particularly the impact it had and was to have on the experience of black women. Complexion consciousness and sensitivity to hair texture, as well as derogatory attention to African facial features—as it is revealed in rhymes, rituals, legends, oral narratives, songs, and fiction—is reflected in the traditions of every venue in which African Americans have gathered, from the pool hall to the house party, the classroom to the club meeting. As a single subject area, it is echoed in virtually every communication outlet used by African Americans. Using literature and oral traditions (including folk customs, folk music, folk poetry, rituals, and colloquial expressions), this chapter anticipates the study of complexion consciousness in black Washington, D.C., by first considering, more generally, how complexion, phenotype, and hair texture have been acknowledged, satirized, and memorialized in black life.

Within African American humor—particularly jokes, tall tales, "lies," and folk parables—exists a sophisticated system of evoking laughter to negotiate racism. These forms are aggressively self-effacing, and in creation myths blackness is often the consequence of disregard for God's law: blacks arrive to be assigned color on "colored folks' time," thus angering God. Black skin is a punishment. Such lore can serve to disable stereotypes by assigning them comedic functions established within the social context of black community tradition, but even as blacks claim the right to name the cause of their blackness, reverberating throughout and underlying such tales are disturbing critiques of black bodies—black skin, black hair, black features— as this "lie" collected from a Virginian ex-slave demonstrates:

Once upon a time you see, ev'y person on God's green earth was black. But news got roun' dat [there] was pond of water, or a lake or something somewhere an' dat if you went into dat pond of water, why you come out white. Well, I don't reckon de niggers was getting long no worse den de niggers and white folks now, but dey want to change [themselves] like dey always has. Anyway, de niggers started a flockin' to di place an' dem dat git dar [first] was washed . . . white an' de kinks was washed out of dey hair. Den de niggers started comin' so fast dat the water started goin' . . . [The water] was almost gone so dey was coming out kinda yellow an' dey named 'em mulatters. Some of de kinks was washed out of dey hair.

Den news come dat de water was almost gone, so dat time all de niggers had got dere, an' dey was so many dat hit won' 'nough water fo' 'em all to wash in, so dey gits down on dey hands and feets an' walked di way tryin' to git white. But de water [only] cover dey hands and feet so dey come out wid de inside of dey hands white, an' underneath dey feets white an' de rest of 'em black. [Now,] when de whites has chillun by de blacks . . . dey might be any color from noon to midnight.[2]

According to Joseph E. Holloway, those who use this story as a way to illuminate the ill treatment and degradation of blacks may miss the tribute to African heritage spoken by this black speaker. As Holloway notes, the tale begins by asserting, rather strongly, that the first people were black, and the story ends by asserting that black people are free from the influence of white blood, with the small exceptions of the palms of their hands and the soles of their feet.[3] There are several versions of this story—an almost identical version appeared in 1883 in Joel Harris's *Nights with Uncle Remus*. In folklorist J. Mason Brewer's *American Negro Folklore*, a black child receives the following story in response to the question "Why is the Negro black?":

Well, God sent Gabriel to get de colored folks an' dey hunted all over till dey found 'em all stretched out 'sleep on de grass under de tree of life. So dey woke 'em an' shove one another, so God hollered, "Git back!" An' dey misunderstood him an' thought he said "Git black" an' dey been black ever since.[4]

In her autobiography, *Dust Tracks on a Road,* Zora Neale Hurston recounts a similar story. She recalls that hearing this tale of race differences "pleased me more than what I learned about race derivations later on in Ethnology":

> So then one day [God] said, "Tomorrow morning, at seven o'clock *sharp,* I aim to give out color. Everybody be here on time" . . . So He looked over to his left and moved His hands over a crowd and said, "You's yellow people!" . . . He looked at another crowd, moved His hand over them and said, "You's red folks!" . . . He looked towards the center and moved His hand over another crowd and said, "You's white folks!" . . . Then God looked way over to the right and said, "Look here Gabriel, I miss a lot of multitudes" . . . So Gabriel run off and start hunting around. Way after while he found the missing multitudes lying around on the grass by the Sea of Life, fast asleep. . . . So as the multitudes heard [Gabriel] they all jumped up and went running towards the throne hollering, "Give us our color. . . ." So God said, "Here! Here! Git back! Git back!" But they was keeping up such a racket that they misunderstood Him, and thought He said, "Git black!" So they just got black, and kept the thing a-going. [5]

Such fictions, transmitted orally without authorship and without an identifiable origin, form the basis of a distinctive American storytelling tradition, one that is, in one sense, extreme in its inflation of the importance of color and, in another sense, frighteningly representative.

Aware of the faint margins and fluid borders between blackness and whiteness, black authors of American fiction have always used novels as an unrelenting discourse in which they could challenge the authoritative posture of the white American literary tradition on issues of race and color. According to Siobhan Somerville, black women in particular looked "to fiction . . . to carve out some space, however marginalized, to begin to reshape cultural constructs of race, gender and sexuality."[6] Beyond the desire to claim a space, writing—even the most fanciful of fiction—paved the way for self-representation so that writing became a necessity, a social and political weapon. It was in literature that a discourse for discussing color, hue, and race could be constructed earnestly and honestly, and black writers could exploit the hypocrisies of American racial categories created by white anthropologists and sociologists. In his 1918 "study" *The Mulatto in the United*

States, white sociologist Edward Byron Reuter outlined the following series of racial categories:

Mulatto	Negro and white
Quadroon	mulatto and white
Octoroon	quadroon and white
Cascos	mulatto and mulatto
Sambo	mulatto and Negro
Mango	sambo and Negro
Mustifee	octoroon and white
Mustifino	mustifee and white

Mixed blood, according to Reuter—whatever the amount of it—"is a problem."[7] To tolerate any amount of race mixture is to ignore the singular superiority of "white" and the absolute inferiority of "black," because people of color, according to Reuter, "regardless of color or training, would never be in any social organization of cultured white people anywhere in America."[8] Even as Reuter wrote these words, white had become black, and black had become white, completely obscuring the possibility (assuming it ever existed) of building, securing, and maintaining racial borders. The most popular and familiar racial delineation is the mulatto. The word *mulatto* originated in sixteenth-century Spain. A derivative of the word *mule,* it is a derogatory but commonly used reference to the offspring of a black (African) parent and a white (European) parent.[9] The character type that came to be defined as the "tragic mulatto" embodied the social threat of race mixing: the "white blood" represented the possibility of civility, which was thwarted by the inclination toward savagery, a derivative of the "black blood." Thus the tragic mulatto, at first a private obsession of whites, was made a public preoccupation by popular white writers, whose works confirmed whites' anxieties about racial mixing by depicting such amalgamation as the cause of national discord and chaos. According to scholar Mary Dearborn, the tragic mulatto trajectory "demands that the mulatto woman desire a white lover, but, in the end, either die . . . or return to the black community."[10] As the inverse of the "mammy mythology" (illustrated by a large, dark-complexioned, asexual, maternal figure), the mulatto figure was "yellow" in complexion, curvaceous and exotic, promiscuous and under-domesticated, overtly sexual, and untamedly primitive. She was fatal, first, to herself. Her image, as well as her historical evolution in literature and lore, worked to exonerate white men from a legacy of sexual brutality by asserting that, all at once, black women could be sexually loose (the tragic mulatto) and grotesquely nonsexual and undesirable (the mammy). In the literature of black women—where the subject *is* black women—this tradition is amended, challenging both the historical sincerity and heroism of white men, the historical obliviousness of white women, and the presumed insouciance of black women. In the work of black male writers, the myth of the primitive mulatto is generally sustained, though it is more carefully ascribed to the mulatto being a "cruel father's child," thus possessing a "love of justice that stirs . . . up . . . hate, a warring Ishmaelite unreconciled."[11]

White author T. S. Stribling's novel *Birthright* (1922) presented racial ambiguity as a black-and-white question that threatened to upset the necessary boundaries between the races (as whites imagined it) that were established through slavery. The book's title confirmed the white right to privilege. Given this agenda, it became necessary for Stribling's black characters to create arguments for their own disadvantage. They name their "worthless" community "Niggertown," *their* birthright. When Captain Renfew, the white protagonist, entrusts his home to Peter, a mulatto and the central character, it is because he imagines that Peter's "white blood" is indicative of trustworthiness and honesty. The Captain soon learns that Peter and his "stuck-up yellow fly-by-night" girlfriend are no more than fair-skinned "he- and she-niggers" who cannot be trusted. He does not discover this through his own experience with Peter but from the black community (especially an old local woman named Rose), which feels hatred of and distrust for their own:

> The verjuice which old Rose had sprinkled over Peter and Cissie by calling them "he-nigger" and "she-nigger" somehow. . . animalized them . . . Rose's speech was charged with such contempt for her own that it placed the mulatto and the octoroon down with apes and rabbits.[12]

Widely published and popular literature by white American authors through the late nineteenth and twentieth centuries has often advanced the belief that is signified by visible difference; in cases where visible is blurred, "blackness" will inevitably be betrayed by the insuppressible brutishness that results from African blood lineage. In Stribling's telling, the mulatto, by the insistence of his own people and against the efforts of whites to identify with him, is as savage, by nature and nurturing, as "full-blooded" blacks. Against their white blood, which "struggl[es] to stand up," is their black lineage, which kept them "buried here in Niggertown."[13]

The problem of color is the problem of imagining that any person of any skin tone can be boxed into a nonnegotiable identity. Thus, passing—leaving the black community to assume a white identity in a white community—is negotiating a level of racial fluidity using physical whiteness and, more important, the *idea* of whiteness as a social identity. Nella Larsen, herself the daughter of a Danish mother and a black West Indian father, explored this through two popular novellas, *Quicksand* (1928) and *Passing* (1929), which speak to the tragedy thought to accompany mixed heritage, the complications of racial ambiguity, and the negotiation of blackness within black and white communities. Larsen first published *Quicksand*, the story of Helga Crane, a classic tragic mulatto. *Passing* is the tale of childhood friends, one of whom decides to pass for white in adulthood. Clare Kendry, the one who passes, is described as "pale [with] gold hair . . . her lips, painted a brilliant geranium-red were sweet and sensitive. A tempting mouth . . . the ivory skin had a peculiar soft lustre."[14] She is, in the words of one critic, "the anguished victim of a divided heritage. Mathematically they work it out that [her] intellectual striving and self-control come from [her] white blood, and [her] emotional urgings, indolence and potential savagery come from [her] Negro blood."[15] This careful construction of identity became the "portal," as it were, through which black women writers (some of whom, like Larsen, were themselves racially mixed) could transform their mulatto protagonists into a class of assertive, socially sophisticated, upper-middle-class women who exercised and cultivated a self-determination that was unavailable to most black women.

Perhaps no woman writer of the Harlem Renaissance perfected this so well as Jessie Redmon Fauset. A highly educated and well-traveled daughter of wealthy black Philadelphians, Fauset entered easily into black Washington's upper-class community, teaching Latin and French at the famous M Street School. Her experiences in Philadelphia, Washington, and later Harlem resulted in a body of work that speaks to the methods used by fair-skinned mulatto women to break social borders, most prominently in *Plum Bun* (1929) and *The Chinaberry Tree* (1931). In the work of Larsen and Fauset, characters of mixed heritage generally pass through white communities, then return to the safety of a black community for several reasons: first, to settle a longing to reconnect with family and "black life"; second, to be free of the constant fear of detection; and third, to escape physical and mental destruction that would result from being "discovered."

Subsequent color designations were a relatively easy way to conventionalize degrees of blackness and whiteness. The historical representation of the octoroon by both black and white authors has resulted in a rather romantic history, wherein the octoroon woman is "kept" by white men but educated and cared for in her own (colored) community, where she is admired for her beauty and her ability to secure the financial support of white men. According to the romanticized mythology, her gentle and refined demeanor and her intelligence are the evidence of the predominance of white heritage; this is profoundly problematized by her slight inclination toward savagery, the result of her "black blood." Dion Boucicault's *The Octoroon; or, Life in Louisiana* (1851), for example, is the story of Zoe, a handsome octoroon woman, a desirable wife in all regards were she not "poisoned" by a drop of black blood—the "ineffaceable curse of Cain"—which she feels compelled to reveal to her white suitor. She says,

> Of the blood that feeds my heart, one drop in eight is black—bright red as the rest may be, that one drop poisons all the flood; those seven bright drops give me love like yours—hope like yours—ambition like yours—life hung with passions like dew-drops on the morning flowers; but the one black drop gives me despair, for I'm an unclean thing—forbidden by the laws— I'm an Octoroon![16]

Several short autobiographical works by women who self-identified as octoroons found attentive audiences, including Louisa Picquet's *The Octoroon: A Tale of Southern Slave Life* (1861), Maria Louise Pool's "Told by an Octoroon" (1870), and Louise Burgess-Ware's "Bernice the Octoroon" (1903). The majority of these works were serialized in popular magazines, including *Harper's* and the *Colored American*.

Who was the quadroon? What was her distinct historical location? How was she distinguishable from other racial classifications?[17] In *The Quadroone; or St. Michael's Day*, Joseph Holt Ingraham describes her as one whose blood is four parts European and one part African. This amalgamation is expressed in the French words Quatre et une or Quatr'une, from which comes the Anglo corruption of QUADROON. Those, however, who retain even a tenth part of the African blood, and, to all appearances, are as fair as Europeans, and undistinguished from them save by the remarkable and undefinable expression of the eyes, which always betrays their remote Ethiopian descent, come also under the general designation of "Quadroon."[18]

The suggestion that knowing blackness is a skill or a craft, an art of detection—and that it is evidenced through the tint of the eyes, or a tinge of olive creaminess in white skin—rests, again, on the idea that, by cultural necessity, the quadroon, the octoroon, and other mixed-race people are—and must be—conclusively and invariably distinguishable from white. I pay attention to this to demonstrate that understanding the history of color-ranking scales as established outside black communities is necessary to understanding complexion legends and lore within black communities.

Stories, Songs, and Such: The Body of Lore

Folklorists working in African American culture have traditionally given extensive treatment to the mining, recording, and preservation of oral lore in every imaginable community setting. Customs, rituals, and folk practices, however, are just as important to understanding African American belief systems. Historically, black women, in the company of other black women, are exposed to folk beliefs and practices concerned with skin lightening, hair lengthening or straightening, and repressing facial features, including milk baths to lighten dark skin, exercises to tighten full lips and retract full nostrils, and home-baked concoctions to straighten hair or inspire hair growth. One need not have extensive exposure to African American culture to know that complexion, as well as phenotype and hair texture and length, have traditionally been important markers of physical beauty. In 1944 Charles Parrish, a doctoral candidate at the University of Chicago, completed his dissertation on ideas about color held by African Americans during that time. Parrish typically encountered the idea that "light Negroes" were approached with suspicion by darker blacks because they invariably believed that lighter black were better and more attractive. He also found that "medium brown Negroes" were described by light and dark blacks as "nice looking and . . . very lovable," and "very dark Negroes" were characterized as "evil and hard to get along with." The names that he collected related to color—from "olive" and "teasing brown" to "rusty black" and "ink spot"—served to confirm the favor that traditionally accompanied fair skin.[19] A plethora of mainstream works about complexion published in recent years—including Kathy Russell's *The Color Complex* (1992), Nowlie Rooks's *Hair Raising* (1996), and Marita Golden's *Don't Play in the Sun* (2004)—have given attention to the ongoing importance of complexion indicators in black life. While these works contribute valuable insight, this study is concerned with contemporary and traditional folklore—lore about complexion, hair, and phenotype—and the way that traditional forms have served to memorialize and affirm (or conflict with) community beliefs and customs.

Without the availability of products to repress naturally textured hair into European fashions, many black Americans relied on folk custom and folk practices as a creative negotiation of American cultural conformity. Some hair-related superstitions are part of a larger body of "pregnancy superstitions," which indicate that the behaviors, habits, and actions of the mother-to-be will determine the physical traits, disposition, and general appearance of the child. "Baby's hair," one superstition warns, "will be the same way the mother keeps hers fixed during pregnancy."[20] Yet another suggests that if a mother has continuous and painful heartburn during her pregnancy, her child will be born with a thick head of hair.[21]

When black hair culturalist Madame C. J. Walker helped popularize the hot comb and invented a hair relaxer, black women already had a system of domestic methods of hair straightening, including the use of common clothing irons and thick, wax-based pomades; unlike permanently relaxed hair, textured hair, when either of the temporary methods was used, reverted back to its original state when exposed to moisture. One cannot underestimate the social importance of hair manicuring, especially for middle- and upper-class black women. This is especially evidenced in the burgeoning business of hair care, the extraordinary cost of visiting hair salons, and the slow process, several hours often, of straightening, curling, and styling hair. In the words of Ntozake Shange,

> Seems like Shelia and Marguerite was
> 'fraid to get their hair turnin' back

> so they laid up against the wall
> lookin' almost sexy
> didn't want to sweat.[22]

With the success of Madame Walker's products in the early 1900s, the business of black hair became an economic stronghold for black women in the form of salons and the door-to-door sale of beauty products. It was as much a means of financial independence as it was a surrender to American standards of alluring hair.[23]

By the mid-1920s, Central Brass Straightening and Drying Combs had made a small fortune selling hot combs to black women. Even later—in the 1970s, for example—and even with the popularity of the Afro, natural hair was less radical than it was reactionary, an option for and a statement by black men and women who were, at once, constructing and reconstructing beauty images. By the time Afros became popular, African Americans were involved in the process of "patterning of culture," that is, altering prominent elements of traditional (black) culture and "putting on" the customs of the alien group, so that the former (the Afro) is transformed into a detail of the latter (straighter hair).[24] In any event, natural styles provided a historical reprieve for hair that had been, in the words of George Wolfe, "fried, dyed, de-chemicalized . . . to death" for generations.[25] Here, Gwendolyn Brooks describes a trip to a black hair styling salon:

> Gimme an upsweep, Minni,
> With humpteen baby curls.
> 'Bout time I got some glamour.
> I'll show them girls
>
> Think they so fly a-struttin'
> With they wool a-blowin' 'round.
> Wait'll they see my upsweep.
> That'll jop 'em back on the ground[26]

Superstitions about encouraging the growth of short hair often suggest that short hair be cut and that the cut pieces be burned into a paste (to be reapplied to the scalp), or that cut hair be placed back on the person's head, or, in one case, placed "in the leak of the house (where eaves drain)." While some have found that placing an eel's skin around the hair will make it grow, others try to save falling hair by rubbing lemon slices into the roots and over the scalp.[27]

Advice for "training" African features has also found a permanent place in folklore. In certain areas it was traditionally accepted that the application of a laundry clip on the base of a child's nose would interrupt spreading, or that pinching a newborn baby's nostrils every day might depress growth. Assata Shakur recalls in her 1977 autobiography that "there was one girl in our school whose mother made her wear a clothespin on her nose to make it thin," and girls who would bleach their skin and "fry" their hair.[28] However flawed the presumptions that govern superstitions and folk customs, they circulate because of the value assigned to fair skin, straight hair, and European features and the equal value placed on folk wisdom and practices. The following suggestions for attaining white skin were collected from black and white Alabama natives:

> Use bear-grass juice and olive oil to make a toilet soap that will keep the skin white.

> To make your face white put buttermilk or lemon juice on it. [Both buttermilk and lemon juice are also suggested as separate remedies.]

> Massage your hands at night with a mixture of lemon juice and glycerine, and wear old gloves and you will be surprised how very white your hands will become.[29]

The paradoxically "white" standard for beauty in African American communities was confirmed and promoted through advertisements in the black press. From the early nineteenth century, virtually every black-published periodical carried announcements that promised lighter skin, creamier complexions, and straighter hair for a considerably small price. Products manufactured to straighten black hair first appeared in African American periodicals in the late 1830s, and just as the popularity of such products was based on the presumption that "black" could become "white," so too the pictures that accompanied the advertisements advanced a standard of beauty that was difficult, if not impossible, for African American women to meet.

Advertisements for straightening products claimed to "make kinky, snarly, ugly, surly hair become soft, silky, smooth, straight, long and easily handled."[30] Other ads, geared toward dark-complexioned women, invited them to "bleach your skin to lighter lovelier beauty!" The popular beauty product Nadinola—which has since revised its beauty claims—professed in the *Afro American* newspaper (1950) that its "medicated ingredients" would act to "bleach the skin to a lighter shade." The equally popular products of Fred Palmer promised a "skin whitener" that would work quickly and efficiently, with guaranteed satisfaction. These ads generally featured either fair black women or a dark-skinned caricature of a black woman, frowning solemnly and standing alongside a well-groomed, racially ambiguous beauty.

The more important promise of these advertisements was heightened womanhood but not for vanity's sake. Becoming more attractive to men—and thus finding a good mate—was the unstated aspiration, since successful men presumably sought fair-toned women. One advertisement, which read, "Lighter, Brighter Skin: A lovely complexion attracts men's admiration," exhibited an exotic and fair-skinned woman who smiles lovingly into the eyes of her equally fair mate.[31] Black women, by default (given the authorship of black and white men and the social privilege of white women), become the casualties in the public tradition of complexion talk, even as they maintain control of the domestic lore.

Wallace Thurman's tragic heroine in his 1929 novel *The Blacker the Berry* elaborates on the use of such mail-order products:

> Before putting on her dress she stood in front of her mirror for over an hour, fixing her face, drenching it with a peroxide solution, plastering it with a mud pack, massaging it with bleaching ointment, and then, as a final touch, using much vanishing cream and powder. She even ate an arsenic wafer. The only visible effect of all this on her complexion was to give it an ugly purple tinge, but Emma Lou was certain that it made her skin less dark.[32]

Implicit in these words and in these advertisements was the belief that dark skin was shameful, displeasing to the eye, a phenotypical affliction. In the words of Rudolf Fisher,

> There aren't any more dark girls. Skin bleach and rouge have wiped out the strain. The blacks have turned seal skin, the seal skins are high brown, the high-browns are all yaller and the yallers are pink.[33]

Proverbs have always preserved and memorialized the beliefs and values of black Americans, providing warnings or instructions to the listener, while the very act of transmission enforces, or at least promotes, a particular view of the world. Therefore, that a significant number of African American proverbs comment on complexion is not surprising. The proverb "it is always better to have cream in your coffee" makes clear the social suicide traditionally thought to accompany the selection of a darker person (generally, a darker woman) as a mate. Proverbs by women signify a relationship between dark skin and self-referential sexual language, suggesting that the African attributes of black women—dark skin, textured hair, and pronounced facial features—invite sexual interest by their own insistence. Consider the following lines by blues singer Sara Martin, as quoted in Sw. Anand Prahlad's *African American Proverbs in Context*:

> Now my hair is nappy and I don't wear no clothes of silk,
> But the cow that's black and ugly has often got the sweetest milk.

The "image of 'milk,'" according to Prahlad, has traditionally referred "to the sexual energies of woman."[34] As a reference to dark women, this proverb at once challenges and confirms the attitude that dark skin can be undesirable and taboo and, still, intriguing. The implication is clear: that a woman is easily made sexual in spite of, or because of, her color. Similarly, the popularity of the proverb "The blacker the berry, the sweeter the juice" responds to assaults against darker hues by self-asserting the sexual desirability of a dark woman over that of lighter women.[35] The recurring questions become: Is sexuality generally defined differently for dark- and light-hued women? How are these determinations directly attributed to the image of white womanhood?

In the blues tradition, both rural and urban, the relationship between sexuality—the "nature" of women—and hue is repeated frequently enough to lend understanding to folk speech patterns as they pertain to complexion. While the skin of a fair-complexioned woman makes her a suitable substitution for the inaccessible white woman, it is in her marginal identity—her nonnegotiable place between the darker woman and the white woman—that her image is fixed. So, generally, while black women in blues music are characterized as sexual, as erotic, the fair woman is both the most sought-after figure and, in her proximity to whiteness, the most amorphous, which is represented as fickleness.

In the folk speech and folk songs by men, black women are both the sub-ject of complexion talk and the object of complexion standards. The songs are evidence that among the most pronounced social influences of white American beauty standards in black communities is the archetype of phys-ical attractiveness—the value assigned to long, flowing hair, "delicate" fea-tures, and fair complexion—which has informed a whole genre of folk music and poetry. In *Dust Tracks on a Road,* Zora Neale Hurston points out that in African American "lies," tall tales, and jokes, "I found the Negro, and always the blackest Negro, being made the butt of all jokes, particularly women." Hurston continues,

> [Black women] brought bad luck for a week if they came to your house on a Monday morning. They were evil. They slept with their fists balled up ready to fight and squabble even while they were asleep. They even had evil dreams. White, yellow and brown girls dreamed about roses and perfume and kisses. Black gals dreamed about guns, razors, ice-picks, hatchets and hot lye.[36]

Consistent with Hurston's assertion, complexion descriptors, often deroga-tory for darker-skinned people and favorable for fairer-skinned people, rep-resent a full range of images: blue-black, jet black, midnight, mahogany, ebony, chocolate brown, caramel, honey brown, brown-sugar-brown, high brown, mariney, red-bone, high yellow, yellow-skinned, pinky, peach, lily, snow drop.

In blues lyrics, the darker woman, without the ability to pass through or opt out of black life, and without the suggestion of racial fluency that lighter skin might represent, becomes a demarcation of stability; therefore, a com-mon composition might, for example, focus on a man who accepts the money of a reliable darker woman (who remains in the domestic realm) to attract the attention of a fairer woman, as in the following song:

> Lay ten dollahs down, lay ten dollahs down,
> Lay ten dollahs down, count 'em one by one.
>
> I went down to Macon, an' I did not go to stay;
> Laid my head in a yaller gal's lap an' dere I stayed all day.[37]

While the "yaller gal" is the object of the story and while she is depicted as a prostitute, there is no blatant value judgment assigned to her color (or her occupation, for that matter). The word "black" is, on the other hand, intended to introduce a judgment, in that it is invariably synonymous with ugly, untrustworthy, and ill-intentioned: to sing about "my ole' black gal" is to document, in implicit terms, settling for "old reliable." According to former Black Panther Assata Shakur, not only did "black [make] any insult worse," but "the words 'Black is beautiful' and the idea had never occurred to most [blacks]."[38] That attitude is demonstrated in this song, recorded in San Antonio, Texas:

> Oh black woman evil: brown skin evil too
> Going to get me a yellow woman: see what she will do.[39]

A similar rhyme appears in Thurman Wallace's *The Blacker the Berry*. The song is sung after a dark-complexioned girl "crashes" an invitation-only party thrown by a group of fair black New Yorkers:

> A yellow gal rides in a limousine
> A brown-skin rides in a Ford
> A black gal rides on an old jackass
> But she gets there, yes my Lord.[40]

The above song and the next suggest that the fair-skinned woman is more desired, even though the desire (often involving prostitution) may be less than honorable. The song below was recorded in 1941 in Chicago and appeared under the title "Black Gal Swing":

> Now a yellow gal rides in an automobile: a
> brownskin gal rides the same
> A black gal [will tell you?] an old hay wagon:
> she's getting by just the same
> A yellow gal drinks good old whiskey: a
> brownskin gal drinks the same
> But a black gal drinks sho' polish: she's
> getting drunk all the same.[41]

As music communicates experiences or desires, the singer divulges the extent to which he is enamored with or curious about light skin and proximity to whiteness.

"Passing," leaving the black community and assuming a white identity, naturally found a place in the folk music tradition:

The burly coon, you know
He packed his clothes and go,
Well, he come back las' night,
His wife said, 'Honey, I'm tired o' coon,
I goin' to pass for white.'

But the coon got mad—
He's 'bliged to play bad,
Cause his color was black.
'O my lovin' baby! Don't you make me go;
I git a job, if you let me, sho.'[42]

In order to determine the connection between physical characteristic and behavior—and the association between both and gender—it is useful to consider evidence of judgments about hair textures as it is represented in folksongs. For example, "Tight Haired Mama Blues" speaks to the bad luck that will be visited upon a particular man for his involvement with "tight-haired" women:

I don't want no tight-haired woman: to cook no meat for me
Because she's so tight-haired and evil: I'm scared she might
        poison me
Now your hair ain't curly: know your teeth ain't neither pearls
If the men were asking for hair: you would have a hard time
        in this world.[43]

As Kobena Mercer points out in his article "Black Hair/Style Politics," references to hair in many orally based outlets (including folk music, proverbs, and jump rope rhymes) simply "code" racism, such that the existing categories of "white" and "black" are expected to interact by acknowledging different aesthetic values (what, for example, defines beautiful or ugly hair), then translating these values into binary oppositional judgments.[44] Black communities hear and repeat such folk songs because they are in fact a private negation of race problems through an attempt to live with types and stereotypes and to trudge through them. Mercer further notes that

the complexity of this force-field of inter-culturation ambushes any attempt to track down fixed meanings or finalized readings, and creates, instead, vast opportunities to consider the ambiguous relationship between hair as a commodity and hair as an "aesthetic systems of valorization."[45]

Like folk songs, folk poetry (short, spoken rhymes, usually containing a lighthearted, accessible moral) documents a historical awareness of complexion difference in the performances and conversations of black men, in particular. With the frequent valorizing of fair-skinned women, the expectation of a demonized darker woman is invariably met. Loyalty to the dark woman, a reminder of the ill favor accompanying black skin, promises little to no social mobility. This is particularly obvious in traditional short rhyming poems, such as "You Can't Win, Gentlemen":

> The black-skin gal craves a house an' lot
> The brown-skin gal wants a car
> The yaller-skin gal wants alla man's got
> An' there y' are![46]

Or in this next poem, which still circulates in a number of variations:

> If you're white, you're right
> If you're yellow, you're mellow
> If you're brown, stick around
> If you're black, step back.[47]

What one concludes about the function of folk forms for understanding complexion depends upon one's starting concept of complexion consciousness: I would argue that ideas about color are thoroughly pervasive in folk forms because these forms have the task of using wit to modify densely problematic race discourses of ugliness and beauty into a location for camaraderie, humor, and even a brand of benign endearment. Complexion discourse, after all, is an attribute of American cultural discourse. Folk songs and folk poetry are not merely objective viewpoints, descriptions, and responses: they are deeply encoded patterns of knowledge that organize, or affirm, our understanding of who we are; they signal to us how we ought to respond to our own image, as well as to our images of other races.

Historically, disciplinary knowledge has been called upon to argue the natural inferiority of people of color. Science and anthropology, theology and sociology have been asked to illustrate inherent deficiencies in the African descendant, and the early arbiters of race scholarship in anthropology, archaeology, and sociology formed what has since become a commonplace image of black people, whose attributes are limited to dark pigmentation, jutting lips, pronounced noses, and woolly hair. In the national history that followed this literary, historical, and social caricature, ideas about black images were continuously affirmed, even popularized, in cartoons, songs, and writing (especially in the popular press), not to mention the everyday vernacular that we depend upon to communicate. It is not surprising, therefore, that when the African in America began to construct a self-identity, it was deeply and irreconcilably informed by these common forms, which constituted the description she was given of herself. She came to believe that to be lifted out of the hovel of inferiority, she must become like whites in behavior, in values, and, most significantly, in color.

In beginning to explore complexion as an issue woven into the fabric of American life, a special set of inquiries emerges. First, what specific needs or preoccupations in the black community do the legends, stories, and rumors about complexion address? And second, how do oral forms help us to better understand race and race mixture, as well as black community dynamics—urban and rural, cosmopolitan and provincial? The remainder of this study uses complexion-based stories and complexion lore to examine such questions.

Chapter 2

A National Perspective on Complexion Lore

Attention to the content of the rumors, however unsettling,
merely detracts attention from the function those rumors
serve for those who believe them. Like a scab that forms over
a sore, the rumors are an unattractive but vital mechanism
by which the cultural body attempts to protect itself from
subsequent infection.

Patricia Turner
I Heard It Through the Grapevine

In 1981 a white New Orleanian applied for a passport, only to discover, four weeks later, that she was *legally* black, the result of having an African great-great-great-grandparent. After having lived her life as a white American, she fought this categorization through the Louisiana court system. Though unsuccessful in her efforts to have her racial classification reversed, her case was the catalyst in the most successful contemporary challenge to the "one drop rule," and it led to a highly publicized—though not legally significant—spurning of the long-standing custom. An absolute division between black and white—indeed, the false presumption that the distinction between black and white is conclusively determinable, without exception—has always required an improbability condition: that people who appeared white, when forced to choose, would have traditionally selected disadvantage (black) over privilege (white).[1] In other words, this rule suggested that the conditions of segregation, destitution, and disenfranchisement were the choice of blacks in the same way that opportunity and advantage were the choice of whites.

This chapter will survey stories and lore relating to complexion, specifically ideas about (proximity to) whiteness and (blurring) blackness. Because stories about complexion tests (lore about paper bag tests, vein tests, and hair tests, as defined in the Introduction) are generally classified as legends or rumors, it is impossible to locate origins. I would argue, however, that these tests were fueled by earlier or concurrent traditions of testing racial borders; three forms, in particular, warrant discussion.

The first "complexion tests" were racial confrontations executed by whites to keep fair blacks from "passing into" white organizations and institutions, including white families. Many early works by American writers make reference to "nail tests," wherein the racial purity of a white baby, for example, could be established by examining the child's nail beds. According to this belief, black blood is evidenced by a purplish semicircle on the nail beds of a person of color. In *A Long Way from Home* (1937), Claude McKay defines it as the "finger nail theory of telling a near-white from a pure-white" through the location of a "half moon" on the base of the nail. He states,

> Walter White, the present secretary of the National Association for the Advancement of Colored People . . . was traveling on a train on his way to investigate a lynching in the South. The cracker said, "There are many yellow niggers who look white, but I can tell them every time . . . by looking at their finger nails. . . . Now, if you had nigger blood, it would show here on your half-moons!"[2]

As writer Nella Larsen suggests in her 1929 novel *Passing,* white folks claimed an ability to distinguish the races by "the most ridiculous means," including "finger-nails, palms of hands, shapes of ears, teeth," and other superficial indicators.[3] Even earlier, in *Senator North,* published in 1900, a mulatto girl's blackness is betrayed by "a faint bluish stain at the base of the nails." Indeed, the author states, "the nails are the last stronghold of negro [*sic*] blood."[4] Similarly, Frances Parkinson Keyes's *Crescent Carnival* (1942) suggests that fingernails are the "greatest giveaway" of Negro blood, even when evidence of blackness cannot be located in hair, skin, or facial features.[5] During one infamous court case in Arkansas, a judge even required a man to exhibit his bare feet in order to establish whether he was black or white.[6]

Other tests perpetrated by whites included the examination of hair roots (in the novel *The Bent Twig*, it is referred to as "the telltale kink in the fair hair"[7]), or looking for a brown tint in the eyes of someone assuming a white identity. In the 1930s a Kansas couple, self-identifying as a black couple, was fined one thousand dollars after the judge declared the wife white upon an examination of her long blond hair. In fact, the woman was biracial: her father was known to be a white Louisiana judge.[8] All of these "tests" depend on the presumption that whiteness is a conclusive category, and they support the notion that there is, invariably, a bodily trait (nails, hair roots, eyes, or even blue veins) that will betray racial heritage.

The second form of tests solicited the assistance of blacks to identify members of the black community who were passing into white communities. From the 1920s until the 1940s, white establishments occasionally employed blacks to work as "spotters," individuals who stood at the entrance to white establishments to keep blacks who appeared white from passing into "white only" public places. The spotters came from the black community, so it was presumed that they were in possession of an instinctive ability to identify "their own" or, at the very least, that they would recognize people they had seen living in black communities. While there is no way to determine with any degree of certainty when rumors of complexion tests began to circulate in black communities, the spotters emerged after the start of the rumored traditions (and after the publication of innumerable essays and narratives about passing) and existed concurrent to the rumors.[9]

The third form involves the formation of any question of race as a "test." This idea, that any circumstance can be an occasion to test into or out of whiteness or blackness, is as contemporary as it is traditional. It grants greater status to the notion of testing by its suggestion that race can be both proven and unproven in any given time or place. Take, for example, the experience of Adrian Piper, a contemporary black woman artist whose fair skin caused her to be labeled a "racial suspect" by blacks. Piper states,

I have sometimes met blacks socially who, as a condition of [their] social acceptance of me, require me to prove my blackness by passing the Suffering Test: They recount at length their recent experiences of racism and then wait, expectantly, skeptically, for me to match theirs with mine.[10]

Piper notes that the "Suffering Test" is as much a question of class as it is a question of race. Most middle- and upper-class blacks, inclined to have a more inclusive view of blackness, did not subject her to such tests. Instead, testing occasions were limited to interactions with fellow black college students who came from traditionally black (and darker-skinned) working-class communities. In passing the test, Piper found on the one hand that she takes part in the process of building race/black identity; on the other hand, what she *then* viewed as camaraderie, she now considers an act of divisiveness. She states,

These exchanges are extremely alienating and demoralizing, and make me feel humiliated to have presumed a sense of connectedness between us. They also give me insight into the way whites feel when they are made the circumstantial target of blacks' justified and deep-seated anger. But because the target is circumstantial and sometimes arbitrary, one's sense of fairness is violated. One feels . . . ashamed at having been the sort of person who could have provoked the accusation.[11]

I am reminded here of a form of testing related to gender. It was often circulated among feminist circles that Olympic officials once required women athletes to bare their breasts in order to prove that, despite their unusual athletic ability, they were naturally women. Exploitative and offensive, the test described in this rumor (the truth of which I was unable to determine) demonstrates that "passing tests" are about domination; they affirm the status quo and attempt to prevent any disruption to existing boundaries, be they race-, class-, or gender-based.

The prevalence of ideas about testing race requires us to question the social necessity of such tests. What general assumptions about race—as they exist in everyday formal and informal encounters—need to be affirmed in ways that can only be succinctly and meaningfully met by "testing"?

To believe that paper bag testing exists is to affirm an often overlooked fact—that our everyday processes of socialization absolutely require an acknowledgment of some agreed-upon notion of "average."[12] It is in our attempts to position ourselves alongside an "average" that notions of "inferior" and "superior" types are formed. In one sense, we could probably hark back to Charles Parrish's 1940s study of color notions, which found that most of the participants identified the "trustworthy" medium-brown African American person as "average."[13] However, bearing in mind that blacks have established groups that mimicked "average" white social organizations—a mimicry that included imitations of appearance, behaviors, and aspirations—moves our ideas about "average" slightly to the white "right." Consistent with these aspirations was to identify white as average, thus exaggerating the absolute inferiority of the darker individual, who traditionally, in the words of one researcher, "cannot conceive himself as 'neutral' in color because his social environment insists upon the 'objective' facts."[14]

Origins

The Paper Bag Principle started with a piece of lore that I heard at Rutgers University in 1987, the first year of my undergraduate study on the New Brunswick campus. It was told to me by an African American woman in her junior year. It went something like this:

> Everybody knows that the AKAs [Alpha Kappa Alpha sorority members] on campus here used to have what they called a paper bag test. That meant that in order to be considered for membership they would hold a paper bag up to your face and you would have to be lighter than the bag. Of course they don't do that any more. But if you look at most of them, you will see that they are mostly fair. AKAs on many campuses practice this. And at black schools, the rules are enforced even more.

At the time I was not aware that this story was normative folklore, a popular legend that had roots on the Rutgers campus but that was part of an elaborate cycle of legends circulating at almost every campus hosting black social organizations. I was curious about how the story had survived several generations, especially since the lore was transmitted very informally and did not have roots in any official sorority traditions. Determining just how many generations the legend had survived, how it started, and when and where it was most popular are, of course, indeterminable—again, such is the nature of folklore. As a starting point for my project, I recontacted some undergraduate classmates. The first was a black woman who was part of my freshman-year peer group. She said,

> I vaguely remember hearing about the paper bag test while we were at Rutgers. And I think that I did hear about it in terms of the AKAs. But I don't ever remember hearing that it was practiced by the AKAs at Rutgers. I think I might have heard that it was at Howard or another historically black college.

Naturally, I contacted a member of Alpha Kappa Alpha who had pledged at Rutgers in the early 1980s and had served as the chapter Basileus (president) during the time that I was a student there. She is currently a practicing attorney in New Jersey. She told me,

> I'm not light, and I pledged AKA and I did not have any problems that I thought were specific to my color. But I did hear the stories. I am well aware, and many members of my organization are well aware, of the rumors. Without doubt, there are some chapters that, by appearance, would support the belief in such tests. It is something that comes with the elitism of the group. That level of exclusiveness is one of the reasons why I chose not to be active now. But I've never heard about tests in terms of our chapter at Rutgers.

Like many observers of this culture, I was very interested in the nature of the discussions that went on both inside the group and among nonmembers; I was also curious about the historical antecedents that made this legend so believable. I was curious about the historical "devices" that were used to maintain a membership that seemed, on many campuses, so heavily biased toward fairer women that it called rumors into existence. In *Our Kind of People,* Lawrence Otis Graham discusses his attendance at an affair hosted by Sisters of Ethos, a closed-membership black women's group at Wellesley College, a predominantly white, elite women's college in Massachusetts. The affair welcomed elite black students from Harvard, Radcliffe, and MIT. He writes,

> With long, streaked, straight—or straightened—hair flying behind them, the Sisters of Ethos were running around the tall French doors, inspecting college I.D.s as they approved or turned away male partygoers who either passed or failed the ubiquitous "brown paper bag . . . test."[15]

According to Graham, while he was well accustomed to the "rules" of the game and while he knew many of the women hosting the party (and was readily accepted), it was "a bit disconcerting to see them practice it so well against male classmates of mine who were pounding at the doors trying to overturn their quick rejections." Later that same evening, with a shortage of men at the party, "darker skinned guys [along with some darker-skinned non-Wellesley women] were admitted."[16]

In the 1996 book *The Future of the Race* (cowritten with Cornel West), Henry Louis Gates Jr. recalls paper bag parties at Yale University during his undergraduate years. He writes,

> Not long after I arrived at Yale, some of the brothers who came from New Orleans held a "bag party." As a classmate explained to me, a bag party was a New Orleans custom wherein a brown paper bag was stuck on the door. Anyone darker than the bag was denied entrance. That was one cultural legacy that would be put to rest in a hurry—we all made sure of that.[17]

In the years that followed my attendance and interviews at Rutgers, I heard stories of paper bag tests in black sororities from Alcorn State in Mississippi to State University of New York campuses to UCLA. There is little variation in the stories: they all suggest that the practices have been long abandoned, that the organization once required fair skin by mandate, that a friend (or a friend of a friend) had been subjected to a paper bag test, and that experience with the test was one person removed.

A select number of black organizations have been consistently charged with contributing to the creation of legends through their membership selection processes. The sorority most often associated with "paper bag tests," Alpha Kappa Alpha, is without any historical mandate that would support this lore, but the legends make a resounding comment on how this group has been viewed by the surrounding community and the way in which the secrecy of this group (and other Greek-lettered groups) is perceived by outsiders. To distinguish anecdotal stories of pledging games from complexion legends and to record an official response to this perceived history, I contacted the national headquarters of Alpha Kappa Alpha Sorority, Inc., located in Chicago. The sorority neither acknowledged nor disputed the existence of a traditional body of either practices or legends. In each of my attempts to speak to a representative from the sorority's national headquarters, I was told that it was a "busy time" and was wished the best of luck.

The tradition of selecting campus queens on black college campuses functioned alongside the sorority traditions, at least insofar as setting a standard of beauty to which only black women were subjected. One of the more poignant examples of this was collected from a Morehouse College graduate who contacted me after reading about my project in a local newspaper in Washington, D.C. He had attended Morehouse in the 1950s, and he said,

> I remember freshman year, all of the incoming students bloc-voted to elect this brown-skin girl named Clarice Guy as campus queen. She was very attractive and outgoing and smart. And her brother was in our class. Of course at that time it was known that the girl had to look white, because a brown girl couldn't wear maroon and white. They said it didn't look good. Our alumni association said that. This brown girl caused such an uproar that, after she won, the alumni association was furious with us! In fact, we were told that our homecoming dance—where we would present our queen— had to be held off campus.

This was among the most improbable stories of intraracial ill-treatment I had recorded thus far, so I immediately classified it as a fantastic community rumor. But I contacted the national alumni director of Morehouse College, a member of the class of 1951, who confirmed the episode to some extent:

> Something like that *did* happen. In fact, I very clearly remember my freshman year when Dr. [Benjamin] Mays was president [of Morehouse] he came and spoke to us at an assembly, and he said he wanted to address something that he had heard: that Morehouse men would not elect a dark woman as homecoming queen. "If this is so," he said, "this student body is a corrupt bunch of men, more than I could have ever imagined!" I know that there is definitely some truth to that story, although I don't know the details of it.

Shortly after hearing this story, now about eight months into this project, I was approached by a graduate student in my department who conveyed to me with absolute certainty that the paper bag test originated in Appaloosa, Louisiana, at the turn of the century. This twenty-five-year-old woman, who was raised in a predominantly Creole community and who identifies herself as Creole, first heard this story from her mother. She said,

> Back in the day, there was a club called the Waikiki Club that was owned by the Catholic Church. It was a Catholic wives' club. The club used to hold

dances and other events. Now these women were all Creole, but at one point, black people—regular black people—started to go to the club. Together with the Catholic priests, these Creole women tried to come up with a way to keep the darker people out and, also, to determine what was "too dark" to be acceptable. Someone among them suggested that the paper bag ought to be the darkest shade of brown in order to be an acceptable [and accepted] member. That's how the test first started.

None of the other Louisiana natives whom I interviewed had heard of the club, nor were they familiar with this particular story. However, many residents of the Seventh Ward in New Orleans, a traditionally Creole section of New Orleans, openly admit to attending gatherings that were called paper bag parties. Not surprisingly, the siblings, cousins, and friends of party-goers exist in larger numbers than the attendees.

Unlike that of Washington, D.C., the Louisiana paper bag test hails from verifiable community customs. According to a sixty-seven-year-old Creole barbershop owner from the Seventh Ward, there actually were parties pub-licly called paper bag parties, even if one did not see paper bags at these gatherings.

What distinguishes Louisiana's complexion discrimination from other American states was that, during slavery, the state instituted a three-caste society, consisting of the white population, the black population, and the population of free people of mixed blood as a third and separate caste. Racially mixed people constituted 80 percent of the free black population during slavery. As the black population steadily grew and became lighter and lighter in complexion, the three-tier system was a way to eliminate cama-raderie between mixed-race people and black slaves by raising the status of mixed people above the status of slaves. Because interracial marriage was not permitted between mixed people and whites, a system of extramarital unions known as placage emerged. This system permitted white men to keep an interracial mistress, often in a lifelong relationship, living in a sep-arate home. Generally, the agreement was entered into with the woman's parents, and it did not prevent the man from taking a white wife and rais-ing a respectable family.[18]

White men would have an opportunity to meet mixed women at New Orleans's famous quadroon balls, where, as Arna Bontemps noted, "upper-class Creoles met and made matches with fair colored girls who had been reared and well educated just for such careers."[19] The traditional three-caste system in Louisiana and the division of neighborhoods by caste after the Emancipation Proclamation had the effect of creating a pattern of complexion discrimination that was organized and systematic in ways that did not exist in other states.

An informant from New Orleans offered a testimony that explains, in some detail, how the actual paper bag event transpired:

> It's like the social amenities. You would not go to a place and somebody would have a paper bag. It's like you wouldn't belch at the table. Now there were some people—just like there are some people who will belch at the table—who would go to these parties even if they couldn't pass "a brown bag test." Nobody would stop you at the door and say, "Let's get the brown bag." But nobody would dance with you either. But if you came, they would call that crashing. It was *understood* that it was a brown bag party. In the culture, you just knew it.

Because women might attempt to lighten their skin with make-up, the bag was more often placed against an exposed arm. It is quite revealing that the social faux pas was not holding a paper bag to a guest's arm but attempting to enter the party "wearing" dark skin. The informant later added,

> With the paper bag test, you had to be lighter than the bag to get into a particular party. Everyone in the Seventh Ward knew about these things and my brother used to go to these parties. A.M.E. [African Methodist Episcopal] people knew about it as much as Catholics. Just everybody.

Another New Orleanian, a fifty-six-year-old college administrator, remembered the paper bag legend as follows:

> When guys went to parties in the Seventh Ward if they were not lighter than a paper bag then they could not get in. It was only guys, because men were more inclined to wander off into wards and areas other than their own. This was fairly common with house parties, as far as I know. And this story was generally accepted as truth. See, a lot of people who were mixed were from the Seventh Ward. These light-skinned and quadroon people seemed to isolate themselves.

Because the tests were believed to take place in the "Creole wards," most of the self-identifying Creoles I interviewed claimed to know about parties directly or secondhand (as opposed to third- or fourthhand). However, they were careful to point out that, in reality, most blacks did not attempt to attend Seventh Ward parties, so the stories, when told by black residents, were understandably recounted with hesitancy, or as fragments of various stories pieced together. It is important, in terms of evaluating the function of this lore, to note that the sharing of legends does not appear to be a malicious attempt on the part of black New Orleanians to slander traditionally Creole communities. The stories are like "turf rules": people would stick to their own part of town, and when they did not, they would return home with tales of their curious adventures. (It is important to note that many young children were not permitted to leave their wards, so these stories were shared secretly within peer groups.)

This next informant, a black program director at Xavier University and a New Orleans native, offered this version of the paper bag story:

> I did hear about there being a paper bag test in the Sixth and Seventh Wards. You could not go to certain parties if you did not pass the test. They would hold a bag up to your face. And you had to be lighter than the bag. That was only in those particular restricted areas.

This informant also provided a story of a paper bag test in a private club in New Orleans:

> I've always heard that in the Autocrat Club you had a paper bag test. If you weren't lighter than a bag, you were not asked to join. But I've heard that they have turned it around. You see the clubs only had social power. That's why that stuff isn't so important. They are only social outlets without any real influence.

The Autocrat, according to another informant, was the club most often thought to have a paper bag test:

> The Autocrat Club in the Seventh Ward was said to have a paper bag test. Their power was more than social. It is hard, even to this day, for New Orleans in general and closed circles especially to elect or accept dark officials.

When this informant was a child, he recalled, his older brothers claimed to have attended "paper bag" and "comb" parties.

Many establishments in New Orleans (including restaurants and clubs, both private and public) have also been charged with contributing to discriminatory traditions by requiring a paper bag test for admission. I interviewed a graduate of Tulane Law School, a member of the class of 1994, who said, "One of the first things I heard when I got to New Orleans was not to go to Pampy's, a restaurant in the French Quarter." This thirty-one-year-old native of East Orange, New Jersey, provided the following testimony,

> My classmate told me that back in the day I wouldn't have been able to go to Pampy's because they had a paper bag test. He was telling me that I wouldn't have passed the test. Everybody, or a lot of people at Tulane, seemed to know this about Pampy's. From what my friend told me, I'm pretty sure it's true. I spent three years at Tulane and I can say how color-struck those people were. So I know that it is probably true.

I contacted the owner of Pampy's, himself a Creole from New Orleans's Seventh Ward, who responded to this claim as follows:

> I have never heard of a paper bag test or a paper bag party or anything like that. And I have certainly never heard about there being any crazy kind of paper bag test at my club. "That is just crazy!" I know some people would say. They would call my club a Creole club, and I can tell you that that is absolutely not the case. Pampy's is in the heart of the Seventh Ward on St. Bernard near Broad. If you have been to New Orleans, you know that this is the heart of the city. We get all types of people in here from all walks of life. We are a neighborhood bar.

The Pampy's legend is significant in that it contemporizes, popularizes, and introduces a new generation to a century-old legend by selecting a well-liked and common setting, then resituating it in the past (thus preventing the story from being easily proven or disproven) and excluding details that might disrupt the suspension of disbelief.

New Orleans was not the only city that faced long-standing charges of colorism. Nor did the southern states, with their rigid color line and notoriously haughty black aristocrats, have a monopoly on colorism legends. In New York, the world-famous Cotton Club was rumored to have had a paper bag test, according to a thirty-year-old native of Lutcher, Louisiana, whose mother grew up in New York:

> When I heard about the paper bag test, it wasn't in reference to New Orleans or Creoles. My mother told me that the paper bag test was one of the main

reasons why darker blacks don't like light blacks today. In clubs—one was the Cotton Club in New York—they would use it as a way to keep darker blacks out. I must have been about eleven the first time I heard this.

I also remembered hearing this legend while growing up in New York. When I interviewed the current owner of the Cotton Club, he provided some background on the club that dispels the possibility of such a history. "The original Cotton Club," he said, "opened in 1923 on 142nd and Lenox. It was owned by Owney Madden, a white gangster, and it was a speakeasy where white folks went." He continued,

> Because the place wasn't legit, the name was up for grabs for a long time. I opened the club in 1978 on 125th Street between Broadway and Riverside Drive. The original club didn't allow blacks in, so any rumors about not letting *certain* blacks in can't be true. The chorus girls, however, were high yellow. Those girls were selected by whites.

Stories of paper bag tests in elite black clubs and organizations, as well as in certain black social circles, found audiences as far east as New York and as far west as California. The Eureka Contract Club in Chicago; the Pioneer Clubs of Los Angeles and Seattle; Bachelor-Benedict in New York, Washington, D.C., Cleveland, and Philadelphia; the Iroquois Literary and Social Club in New Orleans; the Brown Fellowship of South Carolina; the Ladies Pansy Literary Club of North Carolina; and national clubs, including the Girl Friends, the Gay Northeasterners, the Links, and Jack and Jill, are all suspected of having been "paper bag clubs." A significant number of legends appear to have their old and rich legacies in Philadelphia, where the reputation for intraracial bigotry in black churches, along with the absolute supremacy of the oldest black families, was more serious than in most American cities. The oldest instances of hair tests that I could locate came from Philadelphia residents, but as with all legends, of course, it is impossible to date them beyond reasonable speculation. The legends are dated, by informants, between 1880 and 1930, but because they are associated with older churches in Philadelphia, this may indeed be a conservative estimate. The first legend was provided by a retired Philadelphian, born in 1926:

> I am very fair skinned. Used to go to an Episcopal church—I won't name the one, but it is one of the oldest black Episcopal churches in Philadelphia

and we used to have this joke on the street corner that when you went through the door in the Episcopal church they had a comb hanging in the doorway, and if the comb didn't go through your hair you weren't welcomed. That was just a joke, you know. And what they were saying, it meant that if the comb didn't go through your hair then you didn't have, as folks say, "good hair." You know how folks say "good hair" and "bad hair." You wasn't welcomed then, because it meant that you weren't light enough and weren't "right."

When questioned further about the classification of this story as a joke, the informant responded that he never had any evidence of its truth but that it was a story he had heard circulated for most of his life. Afterward he added,

> Most of the people in this church were very fair. At that time, most folks who belonged to the Episcopal church were very fair. And they were, as they say, "good-haired" people. They were the elite, you know, of the bourgeois class. Now nothing would be said if dark-skin people went to an Episcopal church, but they might have been made to feel unwelcome.

One Philadelphia native who is a member of St. Thomas—the Episcopal church in the city most often associated with intraracial discrimination—dismissed such legends, stating that while the church does have a very elitist history, many of the discriminatory traditions were abandoned under the leadership of Father Jessie F. Anderson Jr., the church's former pastor, who actively worked to revise the congregation's reputation.

The social history of Philadelphia's black elite, particularly with regard to sharp divisions in worship practices between the black haves and have-nots, would seem to support and even authenticate the belief in such seemingly bizarre traditions. In Philadelphia, as in most cities, churches with large aristocratic memberships wielded power and political influence, and the cost of opening up church doors, of embracing newcomers, was thought to be high. St. Thomas, a church for "well-to-do" Philadelphians, was largely composed of the descendants of the well-educated mulatto house servants. Central Presbyterian hosted a middle-class conservative membership, while at Union Baptist, according to W. E. B. Du Bois, "one may look for the Virginia servant girls and their young men."[20] Consistent with the arrangements of the aristocracy of other cities, Episcopalians and Presbyterians were leaders of the elite classes, whereas Baptist congregations were generally thought to host the laboring class. Notwithstanding the influence of the orally transmitted lore, these congregations were governed by a most powerful force: tradition. So isolated and dissimilar were these groups—in color, breeding, experience, and worship style—that intermixing was an unthinkable assault against custom.[21]

The complexion and hair preoccupations that governed the social politics of American cities were powerful enough and far reaching enough to leave a residue on other nations. One of the most interesting examples in this regard is black South Africa, where the black American beauty standard—which is, ironically, a white standard of beauty—was adapted by blacks and coloreds (those of mixed heritage who constitute a separate caste in South Africa). Mark Mathabane, a black South African athlete-turned-writer, is one of the more vocal critics of the black South African mimicry of black Americans, as black South Africans have attempted to substitute their more "crinkly, nappy and matted hair" for a more "buoyant American" look. The more black-Americanized a black South African became, the greater his social status. Here, Mathabane discusses the implementation of a "pencil test" to determine the texture of one's hair:

> From time to time [my uncle] proudly told me stories of how, in the center of Johannesburg, whites who encountered black men and women with bleached faces, Afros, or straightened hair, and clad in the latest fashions from America, often mistook them for black Americans and treated them as honorary whites. A reasonable American accent made the masquerade almost foolproof. So for many blacks there were these incentives to resemble black Americans, to adopt their mannerisms and lifestyle. And the so-called Coloureds [mixed race], with their naturally lighter skin and straightened hair, not so frequently took advantage of this deception by often passing for whites. But they were rarely secure in their false identity. And in their desperation to elude discovery and humiliation at being subjected to fraudulent race-determining tests like the pencil test [where the authorities run a pencil through one's hair: if the pencil slides smoothly through, one gets classified white; if it gets tangled, that is "positive" proof of being black], they often adopt racist attitudes toward blacks more virulent than those of the most racist whites.[22]

While the politics of hair is highly gendered, the comb and pencil test legends, from Philadelphia to South Africa, suggest a slightly different tradition. Ideas about the value of fair skin and straight hair were most often directed at women; nonetheless, most of the comb test stories that I collected were told by male informants about other black males.

Legends about complexion tests have enjoyed a lively legacy because they are faithful to the belief systems they echo. The undertone of tragedy in all of these stories—including the discomfort with which they are shared—speaks to the difficulty with which social settings are negotiated in black communities, where a single category of "black" bends and shifts under the weight of traditions, emerging to reflect the community's complexity. Folklore serves, first, to confirm the existence of systems of social power; second, to entertain and make light of painful issues by reflecting its absurdity in the nuances of the telling; and third, to provide warnings about the internalization of racism (the formalizing of self-hatred). What black communities have actually learned through the existence of these stories is more complicated, more difficult, and more problematic to determine.

Chapter 3

Washington Society

I've never seen such a collection of black, brown, tan, beige,
yellow, color-struck, bourgeois, bamafied, blue-veined . . .
prim, high-minded . . . unfeeling, go-their-own-way, intellectual
. . . hopelessly ineffectual . . . quiet and clean Negroes in my
life as I have seen moving in confusing circles in and around
Washington, D.C., all on U Street alone.

Ralph Wiley
Why Black People Tend to Shout

It is not unthinkable that rumors and legends relating to complexion and
hair tests would have a vivid, active, and sustainable life in Washington, D.C.
Perhaps with the exception of New Orleans, no city has documented more
thoroughly the complexion preoccupations of African Americans, as represented in letters, club minutes, editorials, and photographic images. Above
all, these preoccupations have been documented in the memories of District residents.

"As long as I have been colored," wrote a young Langston Hughes from his home in Harlem, "I have heard of Washington society": the "pink teas" (tea parties limited to fair-skinned women) and passing; magnificent homes and distinguished families; grand manners and mouths that uttered formal sentences in frightfully correct English. "Some nice mulatto friends of ours spoke of the wonderful society life among Negroes in Washington," Hughes remembered. "And some darker friends of ours hinted at . . . the color line that was drawn there."[1] Though a distinguished and accomplished man of letters in his own right, Hughes, the grandnephew of renowned Washington aristocrat John Langston, recognized the sharp divide among social classes and the importance of lineage in Washington City. He stated,

> Negro society in Washington, they assured me, was the finest in the country, the richest, the most cultured, the most worthy. In no other city were there so many splendid homes, so many cars, so many A.B. degrees, or so many persons with "family backgrounds." Descendants of distinguished Negroes were numerous, but there were also those who could do better and trace their ancestry back to George Washington and his colored concubines. "How lucky I am to have a congressman for grand-uncle," I thought in the presence of these well-ancestored people.[2]

Hughes's contemporary, fellow writer and Washington resident Paul Laurence Dunbar, described black Washingtonians as "earnest actors who have learned their parts well" and who imagined their social lives to be a very dignified and serious drama. In reality, these black residents, in their precise and methodical mimicry of white aristocracy, were, according to Dunbar, "taking part in a comedy of the period."[3] Hughes himself mused, "Maybe I met only the snobs and the high yellows, and the lovers of fur coats and automobiles and fraternity pins. . . . Maybe those who said they were the best people had me fooled—perhaps they weren't the best people—but they looked tremendously important."[4]

In the early nineteenth century, Washington, D.C., despite its reputation as an economically stagnant city, became an appealing settling place for free blacks. Here slavery was not nearly as significant economically as it was in the southern states. And here, because free blacks outnumbered enslaved blacks and because the rules governing slavery were comparatively lenient, steady streams of free blacks began to make their way to the city seeking refuge.

As the number of free blacks filling the city increased, so did poverty and scarcity of housing and food. Prior to emancipation, families of free blacks and escaped slaves lived in cheaply built, one- or two-room structures facing alleys, part of a housing method known as the alley system. Black residents settled in slum areas below First Street that, because of poor sewer systems, were ravaged by disease and sickness. Others lived east of the Capitol along Rhode Island Avenue, a higher-lying but equally poor area. Inferior drainage, profound poverty, crime, and disease made the alleys prisons of affliction that were out of the sight of white Washingtonians. The names of the alleyways—Hog Alley, Coon's Alley, Goat Alley, and Tin Can Ally—reflected the condition of life for many free blacks in Washington.[5] What is more, the alley system resulted in the complete and total isolation of poor blacks. With limited access to newspapers and high rates of illiteracy, they had little awareness of even the most significant events around the city. News was often limited to scandals and gossip reported by those who worked outside the immediate area. Thus, it is no surprise that the alleys were to become fertile ground for rumors and legends about the black elite.[6]

A short distance from the tenements housing free blacks, the city was functioning as a storehouse—a port city—from which enslaved blacks were auctioned and then transported south. The "slave pens" were out of the immediate sight of black residents, often located in the southernmost sections of the city; the largest was found at the corner of Eighth and B Streets in southwest Washington. Meanwhile, enslaved people living in the District were oftentimes permitted to visit and maintain relationships with free relatives in the city. Black households, therefore, served multiple needs: they were a safe resting place for the enslaved relatives who visited, a home for several generations of free or freed blacks, and a dwelling place for extended family. In short, black homes recentered families that had been destabilized through slavery. It was thus important that nine out of ten blacks in the District had their own homes, however humble, and did not take up residence with the whites who employed them.[7]

Barbershops became one of the most lucrative and well-patronized businesses for black and mulatto businessmen. But by 1840 two mulatto-owned barbershops in west Washington and Capitol Hill had been criticized for refusing to shave or cut the hair of darker-skinned black men, catering to only the fairest of black men in the city and white men. Just as black Washington residents were tacitly nonsupportive of white businesses that refused to hire people of color, so was their distaste for such "race traitors" made known. Because the owners of these establishments considered themselves to be of a "separate caste," the hostility of the black majority was not a significant deterrent, nor did it affect business.

On April 12, 1862, President Abraham Lincoln signed an act for release of persons of African descent from enslavement in the District, and slave owners were paid three hundred dollars as compensation for the loss of their slaves. By 1863 manumitted blacks in Washington owned and supported twenty-one churches, twenty schools, and thirty organizations, most of which had been established earlier by free people of mixed heritage in the District.

Black churches quickly began to develop a reputation for discrimination, especially Washington's Fifteenth Street Presbyterian Church, where in the late 1880s parishioners decried the selection of a pastor whom they thought to be "too black" for the congregation of mulatto and fair-skinned blacks, this despite the fact that the church's founder, John Cook, was a very dark-skinned black man. Even in light of growing tensions between blacks and mixed-race people, writer Paul Laurence Dunbar noted that the city had "great powers of attracting and holding its colored population; for, belong to whatever class or condition they may, they are always sure to find enough of that same class or condition to make their residence pleasant and congenial."[8]

Meanwhile, rumors about the lives of wealthy blacks—certainly wealthy by alley-life standards—created a culture of parody among the poorer classes. Through the trading of illegal goods, poorer black residents participated in the culture of showiness and swankiness for which higher-class black Washington was developing a reputation. An occasional fur or diamond could be spotted in the alleys, and blacks in other cities would joke that hunger and joblessness were hardly deterrents to the showmanship of black Washingtonians. Educator Booker T. Washington commented that, unlike those in other cities, the children of even the most deprived laborers in the capital were conscious of the social mores of the upper class; pretense and masquerading consumed the energies of the lower classes. Washington also noted that it was common on any given Sunday evening to see well-dressed black residents strolling down Pennsylvania Avenue or riding in horse-drawn carriages: in reality, most blacks in the city lived in extreme poverty and the haughtiness to which some of the lower class and many of the middle and upper classes were inclined was not an accurate portrayal of black life.[9] Social pressure and public exhibitionism across class lines grew at a rate that was more rapid in black Washington than in other cities.

A growing source of discontent between blacks and whites was the "passing" of fair-skinned black children into white Washington schools. In the early 1900s, the children of Dr. C. B. Purvis, a fair-skinned administrator at Freemen's Hospital who was married to a white woman, sent his children to an all-white school, and black Washingtonians criticized this blatant hypocrisy: though black schools in the District were thought to be among the best in the country, they were still not good enough for children who could pass into segregated white schools. Soon afterward, the children of families who identified socially as black were also known to be passing at the Jefferson School in south Washington. From the perspective of the fair-skinned, status-minded parents, attending all-white colleges and universities was quickly becoming a calling card of the black elite, and attending a white preparatory school would secure entrance into Harvard, Yale, or Oberlin, the choice schools of the black elite.[10]

The rumor mill was fueled by the growing circulation of black newspapers with generous editorial columns. Started in 1882, the *Washington Bee* was so named to represent its propensity to be unvaryingly "sweet" to its friends and spitefully stinging to its enemies. Founded by W. Calvin Chase, a native Washingtonian, the *Bee* was uncompromising in its attacks on members of the "colored elite" and organizers of socially elite clubs and circles. While no member of the Washington elite escaped the reach of his pen, Chase was plagued by the contradictions of his own position. The son of wealthy black Washingtonians, he was raised in a three-story brick home at 1109 I Street, Northwest. The Chase family became members of the Fifteenth Street Presbyterian Church only three short years after its founding, and W. Calvin's mother had a reputation for hosting teas and open houses for the most elite residents of black Washington. Through his wealth, his brief legal career, and his inclusion in the social elite, Chase had a voice in the black community even before he became an official (and sometimes feared) "recorder" of black life. Eventually Chase paid the price for his unabashedness, including five libel suits over the course of his career and, at one point, a ninety-day jail sentence. While prominent Washingtonians could find their names, their clubs, and their affairs mentioned in the *Bee,* there was an unspoken understanding that—depending on the social climate of the moment—those who were Chase's Sunday enemies could become his Monday friends. Changes in the tide were often believed to be the result of monetary exchanges.[11]

In the late 1880s, in the midst of the growing popularity of the black press, six of ten mulatto heads of households in the District could read, while only two of ten black household heads could boast of the same. The influx of freed slaves into the District in the 1880s reinforced patterns of poverty, and while a small number of ex-slaves further established themselves, the majority remained desperately poor. Well-educated aristocrats, with noticeable amounts of white blood, drew further and further away from the darker classes, distinguishing themselves (free people of color) from others (freed people of color).[12]

Three distinct social classes and living areas emerged in the city. A handful of wealthy blacks owned homes in the southeastern part of the District. Middle-class blacks, most of whom were employed as government clerks, formed a "second rank," residing along Sixteenth Street between Scott Avenue and the White House. This broad and well-paved avenue running through the heart of the city was closed to the "third rank," the poor black majority, who continued to live east of the Capitol.[13]

One of the most popular living areas for upper-middle-class educators, doctors, lawyers, and business owners was LeDroit Park, a quiet "suburban" enclave south of W Street between Second and Sixth Streets. Founded in 1873, LeDroit Park was a fifty-five-acre triangular village located on the northern end of Washington. It was an entirely white suburb occupying one of the most convenient and desirable locations in the city. It was within walking distance of shopping and the theater but fenced off from surrounding black communities. Directly north of LeDroit Park was an area known as Howardtown, a black residential area housing a combination of lower-income families and Howard University faculty and staff. Because of the proximity to Howardtown, LeDroit Park developers built a fence around the enclave and hired watchmen to keep outsiders from wandering inside. But life for the white residents of LeDroit Park began to change with the construction of row housing nearby; also, a rise in nearby commercial activity increased noise and traffic. Moreover, more blacks began to move into the Howardtown section of the city, thus increasing the number of black residents living in close proximity to LeDroit Park.[14]

Although a high fence separated LeDroit Park from the rest of the city, there were several incidents of Howardtown residents cutting through the park to shorten the trip from residential to commercial areas. When the LeDroit villagers replaced the old fence with a barbed-wire fence, a battle between black and white residents ensued, and by the time it ended in 1891, foot traffic moved freely through the area. Two years later, Octavius A. Williams, a black barber in Washington, became the first black owner of a home in LeDroit Park; he was followed by Mary Church Terrell and her husband, Robert Terrell. Mary Church Terrell, daughter of mulatto ex-slaves who were hoteliers, and Robert Herberton Terrell, a Harvard-educated Latin teacher and later a judge in the District, had significant difficulty finding a house where "self-respecting people of any color would . . . care to live. [F]inding the kind [of house] we wanted which either the owners themselves or their agents would sell us was a horse of quite another color."[15]

By 1900 LeDroit Park had amassed a small black community. Georgia Avenue, located just one block from LeDroit Park, became the location for a collection of black businesses, black churches, black clubs, and black newspapers. Howard University, Miner Normal School, Dunbar High School, and Armstrong Technical High School, all black educational institutions, were also located in this area.[16] This breath of fresh air, this emerging black locale, marked the first major challenge to the alley system of dwellings in the District. By the early 1900s, the area was flooded by the black elite: the black middle and upper-middle classes then began to expand, purchasing homes around Massachusetts Avenue and Sixteenth Street, a previously white area. According to Paul Laurence Dunbar, for whom Dunbar High School was named, "Here exists a society which is sufficient unto itself—a society which is satisfied with its own condition, and which is not asking for social intercourse with whites. Here are homes finely, beautifully and tastefully furnished."[17] Though spoken with sarcasm and resentment, his words bore witness to the approaching reality of black Washington.

By 1917 LeDroit Park was an all-black neighborhood. As a black suburb, it maintained the same reputation it had as a white suburb—beautiful houses, well-manicured lawns and gardens, and immaculately clean streets.

By the 1940s LeDroit became the most fashionable address for black Washingtonians. The center of the park was eventually renamed for one of LeDroit's most illustrious black residents, Anna Julia Cooper.[18]

Black Washingtonians increasingly impenetrable social barriers included Richard Greener, who in 1870 had become the first black man to graduate from Harvard University. Fair-skinned and wealthy, Greener came to Washington in 1879 to accept a position as dean of the Howard University Law School. W. E. B. Du Bois considered him to be one of the most gifted black intellectuals of his time, and no sooner did he establish residence in the city than he was invited to every private gathering hosted by his wealthy black neighbors (including the Pinchbacks, the Purvises, the Bruces, and the Langstons—Langston Hughes's relatives). He was soon considered a leader among the upper rank, and a "catch" for any Washington woman able to keep his attention. Greener set his sights on Genevieve Fleet, a young biracial woman who owned a brownstone at Fourteenth and T Streets in a fashionable northwest suburb. She was a private woman who attended only select events, hosted very few of her own, and had a very small circle of friends. Still, she was known about town for her statuesque posture, poise, and beauty. She accepted Greener's marriage proposal. The couple had one daughter, Belle da Costa, who inherited her mother's simplicity, beauty, and grace and her father's intelligence, charm, and wit. She spent the early part of her life in Washington. Her parents were too well known among the black elite and among white Washingtonians for her to "pass" into the white community of the District. With her parents' blessing, she set her sights on New York and lived most of her life "passing" as a wealthy Spaniard among New York's white aristocrats.[19]

Over time, the distinction between the black majority and the black elite became evident at local vacation spots like the summer colony founded by Frederick Douglass's son (and named for his father), where fair-complexioned residents of Baltimore and Washington attempted to bar darker blacks. Frederick Douglass himself felt divided concerning his loyalty to the black aristocrats with whom he lived and socialized and the black majority whom he ardently represented. His identification with the black elite was undeniable: in fact, his home in the Anacostia section of Washington, D.C., started a trend among the black "Four Hundred" (the most elite black families) who, following Douglass, flooded the area in the early 1900s.

Douglass attended a few black aristocratic events in the city, while turning down many other invitations. He appreciated the social company of the black elite and also the intellectual exchanges that such occasions afforded him. Still, he felt a political allegiance to the most profoundly disadvantaged of Washington's black majority, who had drawn further and further from the sight of the upper classes. Douglass's sons were to become members of Washington's upper echelon, hosting many elite affairs.[20]

In addition to Douglass's home, the home of Georgia Douglas Johnson and Henry Lincoln Johnson on S Street, Northwest, became a social gathering place for Washington blue bloods and the "Howard crowd." Mrs. Johnson, according to one scholar, was "quite light-skinned and knew of considerable 'miscegenation' in her family background."[21] Henry Johnson, a devout Republican, was President Taft's appointee as recorder of deeds for the District of Columbia. On any given Saturday afternoon, their dinner guests might include writer Alain Locke; Kelly Miller, dean at Howard University; historian Carter G. Woodson; and, when they visited town, author James Weldon Johnson, his wife, Grace Nail Johnson, and W. E. B. Du Bois.[22]

Beginning in 1920, writer Jean Toomer, grandson of the Washington aristocrat and politician P. B. S. Pinchback, organized "literary evenings" at the Johnsons' home. Discussions often centered around Toomer's favorite topics: miscegenation, racial ambiguity, and the status of "near white" Negroes. During these gatherings, Toomer worked with great fervor to sway the other attendees toward his views of race. It is important, here, to mention that Toomer did not learn of his own black heritage until adulthood. Later, from his grandfather's Washington home, Toomer—who was tall and black-haired, with a light olive complexion—wrote to fellow writer Claude McKay about his racial ambiguity:

> Racially I seem to have . . . seven blood mixtures: French, Dutch, Welsh, Negro, German, Jewish and Indian. Because of these, my position in America has been a curious one. I have lived equally amid the two race groups, now white, now colored. I have strived for a spiritual fusion analogous to the fact of racial intermingling.[23]

Against this striving, Toomer felt himself "artistically . . . pulled deeper and deeper into the Negro group."[24] Still, his ambivalence about race and belonging was evidenced in the final writing of *Cane,* as well as in his story "Withered Skin of Berries," a short fictional account of a woman passing in Washington, D.C., to gain employment while she maintained residency in a black District neighborhood.[25]

In 1921 Toomer went one step further and organized a gathering in the Johnsons' home specifically for those who were interested in "the place and condition of the mixed-blood group in this country and, second, to formulate an ideal that will be both workable and inclusive." Johnson, Toomer, and most of the attendees at this "meeting" were fair in complexion.[26]

While black Washingtonians were aware of the patterns of complexion-based discrimination, they assigned blame to migrants to the city rather than to native Washingtonians. In reality, old citizens (or "Old Cits") were as much to blame, but they were in a position of privilege, owing no explanations for their practices or behaviors. Newcomers argued, however, that "while the old settlers are wrapped in the drapery of their scorn and contempt for us, we are up and doing things. If you ask who are the Sunday-school superintendents, or who is the president of almost any literary society, or who originates, executes to perfection, and mans anything credible to the colored people of the District . . . [it] is the newcomer."[27]

The fair-skinned, Washington-born opera singer Lillian Tibbs, for example, could hardly be accused of bridging the divide between the haves and have-nots: Tibbs, along with her contemporaries, formed a social clique infamous for its criticisms of black folk culture. Nevertheless, she was respected among black Washingtonians for offering "cultivation classes" for the masses. Though W. E. B. Du Bois was the non-Washingtonian who received the most social invitations, and he was known to regretfully decline many, he seldom turned down an invitation from Tibbs, especially preceding her performance for Eleanor Roosevelt at the White House, which gained her recognition well beyond the black community. Her family home on U Street became a premier center for black literary events and for black writers and artists who were visiting the city. Those who previously wielded some social power, including the haughty founders of the fair-skin-only Lotus Club, Wyatt Archer and C. E. Mathews, were excluded from "Old Cit" circles because they lacked the stature needed to transcend their short length of residency in Washington.[28]

An irrefutable leader of the black aristocracy was Dr. Charles B. Purvis, a fair-hued physician who was descended from free people of color. Purvis, a chief administrator at Freemen's Hospital, was one of the wealthiest men of color in the District through the early 1900s, and he held a few exclusive gatherings at his District home, to which only a handful of men and women of status were welcomed.[29]

Leaders of the Washington aristocracy also included members of the Pinchback family, migrants from Louisiana who moved to Washington in the late 1800s. Pinckey Pinchback, the son of a wealthy white New Orleans planter and a mulatto slave, became involved in Louisiana politics. Like many of the Pinchbacks, Pinckey was fair enough to pass for white and like some of his relatives, he often chose not to. He married and had four children with his wife, Nina; their sons, who attended Ivy League schools, had successful and lucrative careers in pharmacy, medicine, and law in the District. Their daughter, also named Nina, attended an all-white finishing school in Massachusetts. Many years later, her son, the author Jean Toomer, would befriend Langston Hughes, and they would characterize aristocratic life in Washington City as schizophrenic, "living at the crossroads between the black and white worlds."[30]

The women of the aristocracy included Josephine Bruce, the wife of Senator B. K. Bruce, who was described as a "tall statuesque woman, fairer than many a Caucasian belle, her pale creamy complexion and slightly waving, abundant hair [giving] no hint of African blood," and Josephine Bruce's dear friend Ida Langston, grandaunt of Langston Hughes, who was the daughter of a wealthy white planter and educated at exclusive schools in the Midwest, where she passed as a white student. A third member of this group of lady friends was the wife of A. F. Augusta, the city's oldest and most successful black doctor. Mrs. Augusta's darker complexion did not go unnoticed among news writers: an editorial in the *Spectator* described her as "darker than many of her social circle, but her features are fine and of that regularity which marks the intelligent members of all races."[31]

Perhaps the most successful of the black entrepreneurs was the Wormley family, led by James Wormley. His sons subsequently became the most successful restaurateurs and hotel owners of color in Washington. The Wormleys, who boasted of having been free people of color since the 1700s, secured a small fortune as caterers and hoteliers, hosting many of the parties, balls, and events organized by Washington's black aristocracy.[32] According to Francis Grimke, a friend of James Wormley, "No hotel in Washington stood higher than his; no hotel in the city was better conducted, or was patronized by a finer class of customers." The hotel was frequented by distinguished blacks from across the nation and abroad, although the Wormleys were occasionally accused of discriminating against their own, especially blacks of lower social stations.[33]

Perhaps the wealthiest and most well-known family in black Washington, D.C., was the Cook family. John Cook, who established private schools for black children, founded the elite Fifteenth Street Presbyterian Church in 1841. His sons were George and John Cook, who became, respectively, the superintendent of black public schools in the District and a trustee at Howard University. Believed to be the wealthiest black resident of Washington, the elder John Cook made most of his fortune in real estate.[34] The Shadds and Francises followed suit and became owners of catering and restaurant businesses in the District.

Beyond private business ownership, the trademark professions of the black elite included medicine, law, teaching, and high-ranking government jobs. For women, teaching (mainly at Dunbar High School) was the most common profession of those employed outside the home.

Upper-class and upper-middle-class white Washingtonians were always distant from the black aristocracy, seldom acknowledging their existence. One white resident—John Gray, a Washingtonian who owned a lodge-style meeting place for whites—desegregated his business, creating a social meeting place for the fairest of Washington blacks. For a short time, distinguished black Washingtonians enjoyed the flirtation with congeniality among aristocrats across racial borders, but when the number of middle- to upper-class white patrons began to decline, Gray was forced out of business, confirming for the black aristocracy that integration into white social circles was not a possibility and confirming for well-meaning whites that the black upper crust did not have good standing among the white upper-middle classes.[35]

The leading social events among the black elite were club meetings, card parties, luncheons, dinners, and receptions hosted for an intimate group of friends or for a large gathering of business acquaintances, family members, and neighbors. For out-of-town visitors, a series of teas, dinners, card parties, and small dances given by their Washington hosts and by friends were intended to give them a warm welcome to the city.[36]

Balls and soirées were often the occasions where young, single aristocrats were introduced to each other and where invitations would be extended to continue conversations at private homes. Over time, Sunday afternoon teas—salon visits in the winter, garden visits in the spring—were a chance for private conversation. In the end, securing invitations to most of the upper ten affairs of the season marked the end of social initiation. Fair complexion was understood, generally, to be a standard "membership requirement."[37]

By 1900 Washington, D.C., was becoming a most popular settling place for blacks migrating from the Deep South, and the black population—totaling 94,000 by 1910—included 1,500 people who were classified as "professionals."[38] This professional class comprised more than 400 colored teachers, 50 qualified physicians, 10 dentists, more than 90 ministers, and some 30 lawyers.[39]

In the earlier part of the twentieth century, black migrants might have chosen Washington over other cities for two reasons: it was becoming an ideal settling place for those seeking government jobs, and the public school system for blacks in the city surpassed those of other cities in quality and resources. With an assembly of blacks from different cities bringing new customs, practices, and beliefs, the District's "black Washingtonian" prototype began to form: Washingtonians were thought to be more educated than "typical urban blacks" and more cosmopolitan and sophisticated than their southern contemporaries.[40]

It was during the second decade of the new century that Washington's black aristocracy began to consider Du Bois's "Talented Tenth" ideology—the call to rescue the black masses—more literally. In 1926 well-to-do black Washingtonians founded the Colored Social Settlement, a "community house built expressly for the social improvement of colored people." The settlement was organized by the men and women of the "educated classes" who took up residence in impoverished areas of Washington "for the purpose of bringing culture, knowledge, harmless recreations and especially personal influence to bear upon the poor in order to better and brighten their lives."[41] Located at Seventeenth and L Streets in southwest Washington, the settlement was a sizeable brick building containing fourteen rooms, each housing a variety of uplift programs for boys, girls, men, and women. The settlement organizers were a recognizable group of "Old Cits," including Roscoe Bruce, George Cook, Francis Grimke, and Mary Terrell, all active members of the elite and complexion-conscious Fifteenth Street Presbyterian Church. In addition to providing practical and educational training, participants received daily instruction on "proper" entertainment and rigid "guidelines" for personal cleanliness.[42]

With the short-lived success of the Colored Settlement, the members of the black elite had created an outlet for volunteerism. By no means was this charity meant to bridge the gap that existed between the well-off and the struggling majority. Daily life, on both sides, remained virtually unchanged. As Mary Church Terrell noted,

> If all Colored people look alike to some folks, they all do not look alike to one another, when it comes to drawing the social line. It would be as difficult for a bore or a moral leper to obtain social recognition among educated refined colored people at Washington as it would be for a camel with a hump to pass literally through a Cambric needle's eye.[43]

As noted earlier, most fair-complexioned blacks remained in black locales, "passing" socially and sometimes professionally in the District, then returning to black communities. One black Washingtonian described passing as "falling off a log," to which Mary Church Terrell responded, "falling off a log is a really difficult feat compared with the ease with which colored people in this country are sometimes transformed into white."[44]

Herself fair-complexioned and acquainted with many blacks who passed for white, Terrell recorded the experiences of several people living on the color line. In one such case, a "competent and beautiful [colored] woman" from Washington, D.C., was discharged from employment at a District department store when it was discovered that she was "non-Aryan." In a second case, a young couple, fair in complexion, headed to the Midwest so that the husband, a doctor, could open a new practice. His openness about his African blood was a hindrance, and after long and bitter disagreements, he headed to the East to begin a "white" practice while his wife and daughter returned to Washington, where she continued her life as a black woman. Of this couple, Terrell said, "When I see this accomplished woman and her little daughter who is as fair as a snow drop and pretty as a peach, I cannot help wondering how the husband and father could have summoned the strength and courage to bid them good-bye."[45]

Following the end of World War I, racial tensions were high in Washington, as they were in cities across the country. The bulk of these tensions were felt by poorer blacks, who performed domestic work and other forms of labor for whites and who, therefore, did not have the option of remaining isolated from racial issues. While some white Washingtonians thought of black Washingtonians as a burden to be politely borne, black aristocrats were sometimes imagined as the mediators between whites of the middle and upper classes and black "folk"—a curious and incorrect assumption, given the limited interaction between the races, and given the unlikelihood that black aristocrats would ever be welcomed into white aristocratic circles for any reason, and on any terms.

Passing was so common between the 1920s through the 1940s that the National Theater in Washington employed a black doorman whose job was to identify other blacks. These so-called spotters, who enforced a "passing test" against members of their own communities, had their names printed in black papers (notably the *Afro-American News*), which resulted in some community alienation. In truth, and to varying degrees, this suggested that the black majority, who were unable to pass, supported—although passively—the right of lighter blacks to "infiltrate" white establishments.[46]

By the 1930s the black Washington community had the grounding and social traditions of an old, esteemed society. In a 1938 radio broadcast, activist Nannie Helen Burroughs proclaimed that black Washington had made "greater progress in religion, education, in material advancement and in social adjustment than any similar group of Negroes anywhere in the world."[47]

By the early 1950s, the Hecht Company (a department store), District eateries, and the National Theater opened their doors to colored citizens. With the integration of public schools in 1954, the black elite made the significant leap to white institutions, while the black masses moved into the previously elite black elementary and high schools.

The consequence of this new social order in the District was the maintenance of ties among old Washingtonians and a decline in the rate and centrality of a "new elitism." In an offshoot of the civil rights movement, the Black Power movement redefined "black beauty" to include a broader definition of physical attractiveness. Black Power, a phrase adapted by Black Panther leader Stokley Carmichael, was a call for black Americans to "begin to define their own goals, to lead their own organizations and to support those organizations. It was a call to reject the racist institutions and values of this society."[48] The fantastic array of names that had been popularly assigned to skin colors—including "tease-'em brown," "honest black," "won't-stop black," and "blackout"—was itself a form of folklore, that is, naming lore. It found an audience among African Americans who could, perhaps, tease out of the derogatory intentions and become a celebration of diversity.[49]

By 1965 the number of black Washington residents outnumbered white residents six to one; this marked the first time in American history that a major city comprised more black residents than white. The black elite, those who had not left the city for homes in the Maryland and Virginia suburbs, lined Sixteenth Street in northwest Washington (the "new gold coast") and the upper southeast. Northeastern housing projects and southwestern row houses hosted a black majority. What distinguished Washington's black population from the blacks of southern cities was the serious fashion sense and stylish elegance that was to become the calling card of the black Washingtonian past and present. The infamous "native Washingtonians," those who could boast of old family lineages in the city, had built up an arsenal of characteristics that were reminiscent of Langston Hughes's characterization of the "Old Cits" forty years earlier: cosmopolitan, progressive, and educated. While many, at times a majority, of the black Washingtonians did not fit this mold, the weight of Howard University, of the "upper tens," of Washington's social legacy, continued to rest heavily on the carriers of the District's traditions.[50]

Chapter 4

Social Organization
in Washington

Oh Miss Pink thought she knew her stuff
But Miss High Brown has called her bluff

Quoted in Rudolph Fisher, "High Yaller"

As long as there have been people of African descent in Washington, there has been evidence that complexion, wealth, and lineage would influence black organizational membership, academic affiliation, religious denomination, and community living arrangements.

Before emancipation, the tradition of complexion-based elitism among blacks was formal, well organized, and of dire social consequence in the District. By the mid-1800s, two social clubs emerged in the city to establish, for the first and for a lasting time, a divide between those who identified as "mulatto" and the black majority: they were called the Monocan Club and the Lotus Club.[1]

The birth of the Lotus Club came through the emergence of the Freedmen's Savings Bank, a banking chain created by black and white northerners to help provide economic stability to freed blacks in the border and southern states. Mulattoes, who had greater access to education and some social leverage (many were graduates of the well-respected Philadelphia High School in Washington), found themselves in positions of leadership in the banks.[2] The earliest black clerks of the Freedmen's Savings and Trust Company established a closed-membership bank ring, which evolved into the Lotus Club, a members-only organization limited to fair-skinned men.[3]

As it grew in numbers, the Lotus Club sought racially mixed bellmen, servants, and waiters who were affiliated with the Freedmen's Bank. In the 1860s, as the Lotus Club began to define itself publicly as a "mulatto organization," W. E. Mathews, a wealthy banker who advocated for the right of mulattoes to identify as a separate race and higher caste, was the obvious choice to be granted leadership of the group. Mathews was able to secure a loyal and steady following and was referred to by members as "captain general" and "lord dictator."[4]

The son of a racially mixed Baltimore family, Mathews was generally received among the social elite in both Washington and Baltimore, and his reputation as a lucrative property owner in the District was preceded by his success as a lawyer, broker, and financier. The coleader of the Lotus Club, Wyatt Archer, was more of a socialite than Mathews, who tended to be more private. Archer frequently hosted events at his home at Seventeenth and P Streets, gatherings that, in turn, guaranteed him entrance to black social events in the city and a place on the board of the all-black Washington Conservatory of Music alongside such men as W. E. B. Du Bois. As leaders of the Lotus Club, Wyatt and Mathews were responsible for regulating membership, and they made no apologies for the primary requirement: light complexion.[5]

Because of its reputation for introducing hue-based discrimination into the city, black Washingtonians felt that the Lotus Club and its separatist agenda were the work of nonnative Washingtonians—black aristocrats from other cities who brought colorism to the city. While black Washingtonians charged mulatto sects with self-isolation, they also believed that these sects did not consist of the native fair-hued blacks. While classism was recognized among black Washingtonians, the complex relationship between wealth, complexion, and social placement was thought to be the consequence of migration.[6]

Among the organizations impacted by the migration of old southern aristocrats was the Fifteenth Street Presbyterian Church, once a meeting place of native Washingtonians of different hues, which had been "seized by [southern] strangers."[7] The result was a congregation of the city's fairest blacks.[8] The Fifteenth Street Church was referred to by outsiders as a "blue vein" church. This term, used interchangeably with the term "blue bloods," was commonly used in white communities to refer to the purity of the family line. Black communities shared this meaning; however, the term "blue vein" also suggested that one's skin was light enough that one's veins were visible on one's arm.

Native Washingtonians claimed that true aristocracy was not determined by membership in the Lotus Club but by the family of which one was a member. Black Washingtonians in the upper tens believed that the only group of blacks in the city who reserved the right to "closed membership" was the impenetrable and insular circle of the oldest black families. According to Paul Laurence Dunbar, "One from beyond the city limits would be no more able to secure admission or recognition without a perfect knowledge of his social standing in his own community than would [a] butler come into an Astor ball."[9] The black majority of Washingtonians, of all classes and backgrounds, tended to demonstrate allegiance, at best—and indifference, at worst—to the oldest black families of the city, and they shared with the "Old Cits" a distrust of the wealthy newcomers. (Not surprisingly, they received no acknowledgment from either group.)

District newspapers in the 1880s referred to the Lotus Club as a "blue vein" society. Blue vein "testing" had its supposed origin in the Lotus Club and similar late-nineteenth-century organizations. As the black press became a thorn in the side of the new aristocracy, that group's reputation as discriminatory and irresponsible served to solidify the standing of the old families. The *Washington Bee* described the Lotus Club as a "disgrace to the community," a bunch of snobs who attempted to hold other moneyed families in check, thus preempting internal reform and aid to the lowest classes.[10] The most ardent opponent of the Lotus Club was John P. Sampson, editor of the

Colored Citizen and a Howard University professor, who publicly asserted that the lethargic state of black life across the country—the limited progress that was being made on the eve of a new era—was the fault of this collective and others like it. "It was the bank ring," concurred the *Washington Bee*, "that killed the era; it was the bank ring that caused thousands of colored people throughout this country to suffer."[11]

In style and structure, the Lotus Club emulated the Brown Fellowship Society, a group formed in 1844 in South Carolina by free mulattoes that discriminated against darker blacks; in fact, the name "Brown Fellowship" was believed to distinguish these brown men from black men. Another South Carolina group, the Humane Brotherhood, was founded, as its name suggests, in response to the blatant discrimination of the Brown Fellowship, but its competitive spirit and selective membership criteria eventually made it as discriminatory as its nemesis. A women's club called the Brownies emerged shortly thereafter. Mary Terrell suggested that the "social functions of this club are always noted for the originality of their conception and the cleverness with which the conceits are executed."[12] As Terrell's description of the club suggests, the club's social objectives were nebulous: that their name reflects a distinction between "black" and "brown" is without question.

By 1884 the Lotus Club was struggling to keep its ranks closed. In the end, the group surrendered to the pressure to broaden its membership, and members of the Lotus Club in its later years included John and George Cook, who were among the best-known and most respected of Washington's native black aristocrats.

Clubs continued with the emergence of the Monocan Club, which grew out of the Cosmos Club.[13] As a *Washington Bee* editorial stated,

> When one considers the cosmopolitan membership of the Monocan Club, it is not strange that this organization has met with consistent . . . success. Here are gathered together some of the most intelligent and most active young men of Washington.[14]

While the Monocan was one of the few elite organizations open to native Washingtonians and newcomers, the club generally closed its doors to darker-complexioned blacks. This was a relatively easy feat because of two contributing factors: first, membership was limited to twenty-five members at all times; and second, members were brought in by family members who already held membership. Families who were listed on the black social register, including P. B. S. Pinchback, Robert Terrell, and Dr. F. J. Shadd, members of "some of the oldest families and best people in the community," constituted the majority of the membership roll.[15] So pronounced was their reputation for caste discrimination that the club was rumored to dedicate significant time and energy to advancing the argument that the racially mixed are "no wise inferior to those of pure blood races."[16]

The four invitation-only receptions held by the Monocan Club were the most well attended of the highbrow black Washington affairs. In 1901 a group of young and fair Washingtonians who had been excluded from the Monocan events organized their own collective. Their events were as exclusive as those of the Monocan Club; however, members of the younger set were creating a new style and social personality and redefining the face of elitism in the city.[17]

Most of the elite black clubs in Washington had limited association with exclusive black clubs in other cities. A smaller closed-membership organization, the Diamond Club of Washington, D.C., was affiliated with the exclusive "Ugly Club" of Philadelphia, and both boasted of memberships composed primarily of wealthy and prestigious racially mixed men. According to one black Washingtonian,

> To be a mulatto almost always identified you with a powerful white family. Those children had more opportunities. They were sent away to school and formed their own societies in northern cities. Usually they intermarried with other (fair blacks) to maintain the masquerade.[18]

After the turn of the century, black social clubs—like the Kingdom, for example—listed themselves in society columns as seeking members who had fair skin, light eyes, thin lips, and high-bridge noses.[19] Of the newly established, self-proclaimed aristocracy, the *Bee* stated, "Because of their exclusiveness, wealth, learning and prominence, [they] are not looked upon with any favor by the majority of the colored people here." Among the black laborers of the District, whose discontents resounded in the *Bee*, the "exclusive set" was a displaced social circle condemned, as it were, to walk the fence forever, "not good enough for white society and too good for that of their own race."[20] Howard University professor E. Franklin Frazier noted,

> Lacking a cultural tradition and rejecting identification with the Negro masses on the one hand and suffering from the contempt of the white world on the other, the black bourgeoisie has developed a deep-seated inferiority complex. In order to compensate for this feeling of inferiority, the black bourgeoisie has created in its isolation what might be described as a world of make-believe in which it attempts to escape the disdain of whites and fulfill its wish for status in American life.[21]

Less exclusive, yet plagued by ongoing controversies, was the Orpheus Glee Club, founded in the 1870s as a social outlet for a small cross-section of Washington city residents. The club was responsible for organizing well-attended picnics and similar outings that, unlike those of the Lotus Club, welcomed about 150 black Washingtonians as guests. When the male officers of the Orpheus decided to extend the invitation to the annual picnic to include more native Washingtonian women, resistance on the part of the "Household" (as the club membership was called) was vocal and uncompromising as the club, the members claimed, was becoming less and less discriminating. The officers were eager to avoid public discord. With a unanimous vote, the leaders of the Orpheus Club abandoned the general body, forming the Orpheus Musical and Social Club, which was decidedly more exclusive and free to include and exclude whomever they wished. It was clear to the surviving Household that sexism—as much as classism and colorism—was at the core of this debate: while officers were willing to tolerate less socially established women of a fairer complexion, the idea of also including men based on hue was never at issue. The final dispute to be settled between the two Orpheus groups was the membership list: after all, it was the signatures on the roster that would determine which club was the most exclusive. The members all agreed to be listed—or included as honorary members—in both clubs; thus the Orpheus battle for prominence ended.[22]

By the turn of the century, migrant mulattoes were transforming into the first generation of new Washington aristocrats, announcing their "arrival" in Washington high society by hosting elaborate balls on the occasion of the 1905 presidential inauguration. The balls were held under the auspices of three separate organizations, "all enthusiastic to become socially supreme." The Native Washingtonian ball claimed superiority by virtue of the number of "Old Cits." The Citizens Committee, a competing group consisting of the new elite, emphatically stated that while they did not intend to exclude anyone, "in fact, [we] will." In reality, both balls invited many of the same residents, and, according to writer Paul Laurence Dunbar, many Washingtonians spent the evening in a "good-natured shifting of guests from one ballroom to another." The *Washington Bee,* in response to the evening's events, said, "If there could be one inaugural ball among colored society, what an event it would be."[23]

Of the clubs organized by black Washingtonians, "there is none," according to Mary Church Terrell, "more interesting than the Pen and Pencil Club, which is composed of some of the cleverest and most intellectual men of the race." The club comprised men who pushed pens and pencils for a living, including writers, publishers, and contributors to black magazines and newspapers. It was less elite, in terms of complexion, than Lotus and other restricted clubs.[24]

Cries against intraracial ill-treatment were occasionally heard from within the ranks of the elite. As Nannie Helen Burroughs, a race leader and honorary member of the Washington set, put it, "There is no denying it, Negroes have color-phobia. Whole Negro communities have it. Some Negro families have it. Some Negro churches have it. The fairer some Negroes are, the better they think themselves."[25]

Among the intellectual crowd, the MuSoLit Club became a house of refuge. With an invitation-only membership, the "Music, Social and Literary" Club was one of the few to own its own clubhouse, a brick edifice located on R Street, Northwest. The club provided "respite of a purely social nature from the strife of race questions of the hour."[26] When they were in town, respected black figures, including politicians, diplomats, writers, and artists, visited the club. W. E. B. Du Bois frequented the club during visits to Washington to engage in friendly debates with his peers. Membership in MuSoLit generally included invitations to some of black Washington's choice social affairs. It is unclear exactly how members were chosen for the group; in fact, though the club had as many as one hundred members at a time, meeting records reflect an ongoing debate about the membership-selection processes.[27] Prior to 1920, selection appears to have been rather arbitrary, and this haphazard method led to local mythology about the "criteria" for membership. It was not unthinkable to many black Washingtonians that MuSoLit be counted among the premiere "paper bag clubs" in the city.

Early Legends

Discussion of "paper bag tests" and other complexion tests cannot be found in newspapers, journals, or the writings of Washingtonians; it is only recorded through the oral history of Washington families, migrants, and visitors to the city.

One of the first stories about colorism in Washington was told to me by a Nashville, Tennessee, native who came to Washington in the late 1930s. She recounted the story about the son of a well-respected Washington pharmacist who was excluded from a private party after failing a paper bag test. "He was chocolate brown," she said, and as he was about to be escorted from the affair, someone approached the door, saying, "That's Dr. Plummer's son!" Then, she recalls hearing, he was asked to come in. Such rumored stories are without historical evidence; however, the players in this case were real. Dr. Plummer (as the pharmacist was popularly known) resided in the District from the early 1900s and was perhaps the most well-respected black practitioner in the area, although he was not a full-fledged black Washington aristocrat.

The phrase "paper bag party" conveyed a general understanding that an affair was restricted to a particular "type" of Washingtonian. Within this construction, neither a "bag" nor a "test" was necessary, because the term was synonymous with "invitation only." The idea, however, is that the paper bag test was forced upon an unsuspecting victim; of course, the test was generally implemented when it was clear, in advance, that the person would "fail." Therefore, blackness could be categorically "ordered" by the creation of a systematic but rather informal, or undocumented, "cutoff" system. As with most legends, the popularity of this lore has more to do with informal and unexplained exclusion than with an actual system of complexion testing. While there is no shortage of people who have "a friend of a friend" who was reportedly subjected to a "test," actual victims are not known to exist. According to one native Washingtonian and a member of the exclusive What Good Are We Club, "You never really need any test of any kind." He acknowledged that virtually all members of his club are to this day very fair but stated, "We owe no explanation to anyone about why they are not wanted. Sometimes a lot of members of a certain group are fair, like me. And sometimes, that's just the way it is."

Not surprisingly, What Good Are We is one of the clubs in Washington often associated with paper bag tests, but this association is merely a way of memorializing the club's arbitrary membership requirements. Many of the first members of the club were graduates of Howard Medical School who were attempting to maintain ties among school friends who were practicing medicine in the District (my informant was not a doctor). As members of the club moved on or died, a younger relative might be taken in, but for the most part, the group maintained the same membership for several decades. Because the group has no charter, no official rules of order, and no documented objectives, it became an attractive and easy target for legends. I wish to argue here that intraracial ideas about complexion are conceived within the language used to talk about the significance of racism beyond the gaze of the most carefully defined of racial terms: whiteness.

Open-membership organizations such as the National Association for the Advancement of Colored People (NAACP) were charged with "colorizing" or racializing the predominantly black membership as early as 1918. One District resident described the NAACP as "Grimke's Lodge," a private club for the "yellar skin[ned]" that excluded the black majority.[28] Francis Grimke was a Princeton graduate and the pastor of the Fifteenth Street Presbyterian Church, which catered to the spiritual needs of the fairest and wealthiest of black Washingtonians. "That feller Grimke gives me a cold in my feet," a black District barber recounted to a *Washington Bee* writer in 1918 about Grimke and his leadership. "With his yellar skin and white hair combed back, [he] thinks he's better than anybody else." The shop then erupted into a "rapsodious [*sic*] giggle of approval," according to the writer, who responded, "[Grimke] may have been born in Charleston and his daddy or granddaddy may have been some old cracker aristocrat, but he has done more for blacks in the district than they realize."[29] This was the dual reality: that race leaders, even given their practical import in securing rights for blacks, remained distant and obscure to the black masses in color and thus, principally, in cultural experience. In part, this was a reaction to Grimke's church, which, through the early 1900s, was continuously charged with discriminating against darker Washingtonians—a claim that is difficult to dismiss when one views photographs of the congregation.

Local Legends with National Precedents

By the 1930s and 1940s, the black women's club movement had fully taken hold among District women of different social stations. According to Fannie Barrier Williams, the black women's club movement "was not a fad . . . not an imitation"; instead, it was "the force of a new intelligence against old ignorance."[30] Whereas early men's clubs may have been consumed with discussions of the "race problem" and the color line, the women's groups preferred to think of themselves as being community action-based. National clubs with local chapters flourished, such as "wartime clubs" among middle-class black women, which had, as their primary objective, promoting the sale of war bonds. Participation in wartime clubs became a mark of civic duty: black leaders saw the war as an opportunity to bridge the divide between blacks and whites, especially in the nation's capital. Clubs such as the War Hospitality and Hearthstone War Workers hosted a majority of fairer-skinned women, who dedicated long hours to war efforts and bridging racial divides but were limited in their ability to address intraracial concerns. The greatest shift from previous generations was the creation of active nation-wide social alliances, networks of blacks who self-identified as upper and upper-middle class and were officially joined together across the country by selective national clubs. There is no black club or organization in any city that has been associated with "paper bag tests" with as much frequency as Jack and Jill of America, Inc., founded in 1938 by a group of Philadelphia mothers. According to Louise Truitt Jackson Dench, a Jack and Jill founder, the organization was formed by Margery Anderson and her friends during a Christmas party as a way to maintain ties among friends, many of whom had started families and moved to various parts of Philadelphia and other cities. According to Dench,

I went to Brooklyn once to visit a friend. She was telling me what a wonderful Christmas they had had with all their visiting friends who had moved away into various boroughs and cities. They had all these children now and everyone came back and had a Christmas party. I enjoyed the story and I said, "Gee, Philadelphia could enjoy something like that, but I want our group to be a club permanently, not just get-together's at Christmas."[31]

For Margaret Turner Stubbs Thomas, another founder, Jack and Jill "to us as mothers . . . has become a means of furthering an inherent and natural desire . . . to bestow upon our children all the opportunities possible for a normal and graceful approach to a beautiful adulthood."[32] Many of the women who were involved in the inception of the organization were graduates of Girls High in Philadelphia; thus, the social ties among members of this organization predates the women's efforts to organize a social network.

According to one informant, a native Washingtonian, the first stories that she heard about paper bag tests were in connection with Jack and Jill:

I have heard of a paper bag test. That was where if your skin was lighter than a paper bag you were accepted in certain social circles. I remember hearing my sister talk about it in terms of Jack and Jill, but it wasn't new to me when I heard it from her. As time went on, I may have heard it in reference to sororities.

This informant, who left the District to attend Wellesley College in Massachusetts, is dark in complexion, while her sister is fair in complexion. She continued,

In fact, my sister said that she would not join Jack and Jill because she had heard about the paper bag test and she wouldn't join a club that her sister couldn't join.

In *Our Kind of People,* author Lawrence Otis Graham, who grew up in Jack and Jill, described the collective this way: "a non-profit service organization, it focuses on bringing together children aged two to nineteen and introducing them to various education, social and cultural experiences."[33] The original group, according to the daughter of a Jack and Jill founder, was called "Club 18," after the eighteen founding members. After their children all reached the age of twelve, there would be a "promotion" to the second level, which, at the time, they named the "Hilltop Teens." The third group (upper teens) was called "Ace of Teens." Many members of the group maintained relationships, and some married each other. Meanwhile, other chapters, the second in New York and the third in Washington, grew steadily.

Today Jack and Jill has 218 chapters in the United States and Germany, with a membership comprising more than thirty thousand parents and children. It is the largest and most influential private black family organization in the country. The group is governed by a national office, although the local chapters enjoy relative autonomy. In each chapter, the young people are organized by age level, totaling five groups from toddlers to teenagers, and activities enable children to get to know the members of their group and the occasional new member who will join along the way.[34]

Older members of the organization are less familiar with the rumors that circulate about complexion tests than younger members. One Washington member of Jack and Jill, whose mother was a founding member of the group in Philadelphia, has had various levels of involvement with Jack and Jill for her entire life. She said of complexion discrimination in the organization,

> Having been around Jack and Jill from the very beginning, and from the standpoint of a parent and of a child, I can say that many of the children were fair-skinned, but there was a total representation of hues. I have never heard anyone say anything—ever—about hue. Our executive board also represents that fact that that is not true. They are of all hues.

As the descendant of "free people of color" who owned considerable property in Philadelphia by the mid-1800s, she admitted that she may have been "sheltered from a lot." Her maternal great-grandfather, the co-owner of Augustin and Baptiste Caterers of Philadelphia from the 1850s until the 1910s, transported food by rail to accommodate presidential inaugural events; in fact, a specialty soup of her great-grandfather's was even shipped abroad at the request of French royalty.

Of the paper bag tests, she said,

> I actually did not hear anything about the existence of paper bag tests until I was an adult. The idea was totally foreign—I mean foreign!—to me and

to my upbringing. My father looks white. My mother is brown. Two of their children are very light, and one is brown. We all grew up with total acceptance. One of my childhood friends in Jack and Jill was the daughter of my mom's friend and now our children are friends. They share a common interest in tennis. I think that when there are not a lot of minorities present, you will gravitate to each other. Peer groups will form naturally. And that is what happened with Jack and Jill. They were existing peer groups [not intended to signify exclusion].

When asked about whether the attitudes of native Washingtonians might represent a similar sentiment, she said,

> I would say that within Jack and Jill in D.C. there may have been a natural inclination for the native Washingtonians to maintain the bonds that they already had. A good number of the members in D.C. are native Washingtonians. But, again, that is part of this natural inclination.

The daughter of another Jack and Jill founder had heard about the paper bag test in connection with Jack and Jill, and she said that while the color line did exist, there were always darker members. When asked about the frequency with which the paper bag legend was attributed to Jack and Jill, she responded that many of the women who founded Jack and Jill were fair and had straight hair. Also, she observed, people who were not invited to join might want to find a reason for why they were not included. While there is no question that many of the members were light, she did not believe the stories when she heard them in adulthood.

According to one of my interviewees, who is the daughter of a founder and herself a member of Jack and Jill in Washington, D.C.:

> Typically, new members are recommended. They are invited to fundraisers to get to meet members. Then there is a presentation of potential members, with their bios. Then there is a voting process. The number of people who will be voted in hinges on the number of outgoing members—[that is] the number of families whose children are going off to college [therefore] will be leaving the group. So say there are 120 members, for example, and three families are leaving. From the pool of applicants, three families will be chosen.

Of membership requirements, Lawrence Otis Graham writes,

[M]any parents who are outside of Jack and Jill find the admission process highly frustrating. The way one gets into Jack and Jill is by knowing some-one who already belongs. And that is how we got in: my parents' attorney and his wife, a pharmacist, proposed us in the early 1960s ... the only indi-viduals guaranteed membership are those whose parents were Jack and Jill members as children.[35]

Retrospectively, Graham indicated that there were dual drawbacks of this childhood experience: on the one hand, he lacked any "real sense of the anger and dissatisfaction that the rest of black America was expressing in the late 1960s and early 1970s." On the other hand, and equally disconcerting, he came away from Jack and Jill feeling that he was "somehow disadvantaged" because of the obvious, unrelenting, and unconcealed competitions among children over issues such as house size, the schools one attended, and par-ents' occupations.[36]

To a lesser degree than Jack and Jill, the Girl Friends have also been asso-ciated with complexion discrimination and linked to complexion tests. A longtime affiliate of Jack and Jill, this organization was founded in New York City in 1927 by a small group of friends seeking a formal way of keeping in touch as they attended college in different cities. They defined the Girl Friends as a "social club with cultural and civic interests" and borrowed the name from a popular song at that time. The following year a chapter was started in Philadelphia, ten years prior to the inception of Jack and Jill in that city.[37]

While I did not hear stories about the paper bag test or other tests being associated with the Girl Friends in Washington, D.C., it is generally thought that the organization in Washington has traditionally discriminated on the basis of complexion. Photographs of Girl Friend meetings and affairs, from New York to Chicago and back to Washington, indicate that fairer-skinned women have dominated the organization. But, accounts of paper bag tests can be thought of in two ways. They are erroneous only in the sense that no member of Jack and Jill or a similar organization would ever substantiate claims of being subjected to such an outrageous and unthinkable process. In other words, it is probably true that, in the history of such organizations (in Washington or elsewhere), a paper bag was never held to the face or hand of a potential member, followed by either a congratulatory welcome or a swift dismissal. In another sense, however, the stories are authentic. The fact that, historically, the memberships of such organizations have been overwhelmingly fair-complexioned would suggest that the underlying idea of the paper bag test has informed their approach to considering potential members. Certainly, that is how things appear from the outside. It is this passive application that I have named the paper bag principle.

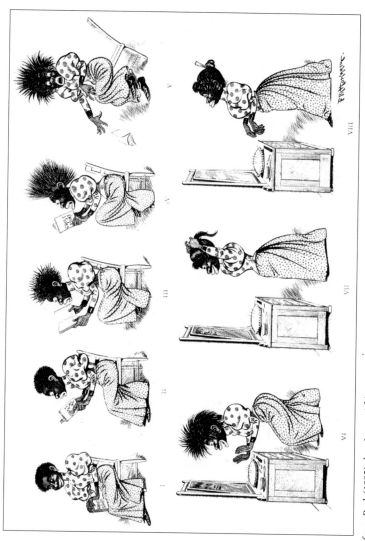

Cartoon from *Puck* (1895) showing an African American woman taking kinks out of her hair after reading a hair-raising ghost story. Engraving copyrighted by Keppler & Schwarzmann, after a drawing by F. M. Howarth. Courtesy of the Library of Congress.

Advertisement for miracle hair grower. *Half-Century* magazine, 1917.

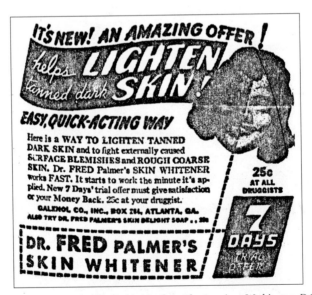

Advertisement for Dr. Fred Palmer's skin bleacher. *Afro-American*, Washington, D.C., 1940.

Advertisement for Nadinola black skin bleacher. *Afro-American,* Washington, D.C., 1950.

Hostesses at a Washington social in the 1950s. Courtesy of the Pittsburg Courier Collection, Moorland-Spingarn Research Center, Howard University.

African American family and their home in one of the alley-dwelling sections of Washington. Photograph by Edwin Rosskam, 1941. Courtesy of the Library of Congress.

An African American doctor's home on the outskirts of Washington. Photograph by Marjory Collins, 1942. Courtesy of the Library of Congress.

Bachelor-Benedict Club, Washington, D.C., 1946. Courtesy of the Howard University Archives, Moorland-Spingarn Research Center.

Bachelor-Benedict Wives, 1945. Courtesy of the West Virginia State Archives, Phyllis Preston Jarrett Collection.

Bachelor-Benedict Christmas party, 1945. Courtesy of the West Virginia State Archives, Phyllis Preston Jarrett Collection.

Members of the Girl Friends present a check to union leader A. Philip Randolph in the New York office of the Brotherhood of Sleeping Car Porters. Photograph by Rufus Merritt, 1950. Courtesy of the Library of Congress.

Executive board meeting of The Links, Inc., in Washington, D.C., 1961. Courtesy of the Pittsburg Courier Collection, Moorland-Spingarn Research Center, Howard University.

Students working in a machine shop at the Armstrong Technical High School in Washington.
Photograph by Marjory Collins, 1942. Courtesy of the Library of Congress.

Ivy Leaf Club, Alpha Kappa Alpha, 1933. Courtesy of the Howard University Archives,
Moorland-Spingarn Research Center.

Members of Alpha Kappa Alpha Sorority, 1942. Courtesy of the Howard University Archives, Moorland-Spingarn Research Center.

The Pyramid Club, an interest group within the Delta Sigma Theta Sorority, Inc., 1934. Courtesy of the Howard University Archives, Moorland-Spingarn Research Center.

Delta Sigma Theta Sorority, Inc., 1934. Courtesy of the Howard University Archives,
Moorland-Spingarn Research Center.

Members of Zeta Phi Beta Sorority, Inc., at Howard University in 1933. Courtesy of the Howard University Archives, Moorland-Spingarn Research Center.

Howard beauty queens, 1942: Charlotte Wesley, Miss Collegiate America (left); Harriet Pearson, Miss Hilltop Homecoming Queen (right). Courtesy of the Howard University Archives, Moorland-Spingarn Research Center.

Mary Settle, voted "Most Beautiful" at Howard in 1946. Courtesy of the Howard University Archives, Moorland-Spingarn Research Center.

"Eye Lights of Forty-Six," page from the 1946 Howard yearbook. Courtesy of the Howard University Archives, Moorland-Spingarn Research Center.

Chapter 5

School Lore: Belief and Practice in the Education of Black Washington

[Students] were either mulattoes or light brown. In southern homes, they had segregated themselves from their dark-skinned brethren. Though they were not organized in blue vein society, they nevertheless kept to themselves. She has a vague idea that [these] people on campus were the only people with whom she should associate.

Wallace Thurman
The Blacker the Berry

Even before black Washingtonians established public schools for black children, even while a battle for school accommodations was being fought by ex-slaves in Washington, even before the dawn of a new century, the question of color existed in black education.

The first black teacher in the District, Anne Maria Hall, began instructing black children in 1810; however, a black school did not materialize in Washington until 1818, when one was organized by the Resolute Beneficial Society. Between 1818 and the mid-1800s, a single high school for black children existed. Called simply the Colored High School, it instituted the same acceptance standards as white high schools, admitting students at a rate of 60 percent. Discontinuity between the curriculum of the Colored High School (which replicated the curriculum in white high schools) and the practical knowledge that black children needed was immediately evident, and the 60 percent acceptance rate created a standard that was inconsistent with the experience of most school-aged black Washingtonians.[1]

Between the turn of the century and the *Brown v. Board of Education* decision (1954), the District educated all of its black high school students in three small, poorly maintained frame buildings; younger black students were served by thirteen elementary and middle schools. Concentrated between North Capitol Street, Massachusetts Avenue, Ninth Street, and Florida Avenue, Northwest, these schools were woefully inadequate in size and resources. Meanwhile, the six white senior high schools were located in expansive buildings throughout the city.[2]

The most prestigious of the black high schools, named after the black poet and Washington native Paul Laurence Dunbar, was located on First Street between N and O Streets. Originally called M Street High School, Dunbar High was founded in the basement of the Fifteenth Street Presbyterian Church, the religious sanctuary of Washington's black aristocracy. By 1916 the school's name was changed to Dunbar High School and moved to a Tudor-style building at First and N Streets, Northwest.[3]

Dunbar was the only public high school for college-bound black Washingtonians. Despite Dunbar's lofty academic agenda and even despite its astounding success, Dunbar's facilities remained inferior to those of Central High School, a school that was "of approximately the same age and instituted for the purpose of providing general or comprehensive academic courses for white [students]."[4] Although, unlike the other black schools, Dunbar had the distinction of not being a "hand-me-down" school from whites, it was a small and costly piece of real estate located in the middle of the city, while the all-white Central High School was located in a quiet, spacious residential suburb and had sprawling lawns, a sizeable stadium, and barely enough students to fill its classrooms.

By the mid-1900s, Dunbar was known across the nation as the premier high school for black students. It began attracting children from middle-class or privileged black Washington families. "You'd see a darker black going to Dunbar," said a 1948 graduate, "and you'd say, 'Gee, you must be smart if you go here.'" Thus, it was often suggested that darker students had to compensate for their color with exceptional intelligence or wealth. "There didn't seem to be any overt hostility," the fair-skinned graduate recalled, "you were just sort of looked on with wonder if you were dark-skinned and went there."

Dunbar's reputation had been a long time in the making. In 1921 three of the women on the faculty at Dunbar had earned doctorates from Ivy League universities. According to a 1938 graduate of Dunbar High School,

> Dunbar was the epitome of good high school education in America. We had five PhDs [on the faculty] at the time. Eighty percent went to college and the other 20 percent who didn't go [probably] had monetary problems. Armstrong was a good school, [but] it was designed to teach a trade.

An informant named Ross, who attended Dunbar ten years later, also attributed the success of the students to the admirable faculty:

> It was post–World War II and most of the teachers were pretty dedicated folks. Excellence was the norm. I'll give you an example of the type of people that Dunbar produces; in 1948 five members of the graduating class became one-star generals in the army or admirals in the navy. I would say between 80 and 90 percent became professionals. It was sort of like Fisk University, where academic excellence was the norm. It was the equivalent of a middle-class white finishing school. And I would say a very small amount was from broken or single-parent homes.

It was the prestigious faculty that sustained Dunbar's reputation for excellence over a span of sixty years. Among the early distinguished Dunbar faculty were Angline, Archibald, and Francis Grimke. Archibald Grimke graduated from Harvard Law School, and in 1905 his daughter, a poet, also became a well-respected member of the Dunbar High School family.[5]

Around the same time, Anna J. Cooper, the well-known abolitionist and activist, joined the faculty as a Latin teacher, the beginning of a career that spanned more than forty years. Cooper had earned degrees from Oberlin College. Later she earned a doctorate from the Sorbonne in France. Among her greatest accomplishments at Dunbar, Cooper used her connections in higher education to secure the entrance of Dunbar's brightest and best to Harvard, Brown, Yale, and other Ivy League institutions.[6]

Students at Dunbar divided themselves into social cliques based on a number of factors, including their family backgrounds and the neighborhoods in which they lived. A number of Dunbar mothers organized their children into small clubs like the "Sappy Sues" and the "Smart Set." A forty-year-old University of Maryland administrator noted that the web connecting Dunbar graduates was hardly coincidental. Her aunts, who attended Dunbar in the 1930s, lived in the LeDroit Park area; they attended the exclusive Fifteenth Street Presbyterian Church; and their social circle was completed by membership in the "Smart Set" with fellow LeDroit Park classmates. Later, most of them went to Howard and married members of their social group.

The social experience of the fairest of the Dunbar students was marked by their ability to "pass" in and around Washington, D.C., after school. It was common for a group of Dunbar students to "pass" undetected into the National Theater and to visit District eateries unbeknownst to white proprietors and patrons.

Intraracially, Ross recalled, colorism was "institutionalized to the point where virtually no one, fair or dark, protest[ed] it." He added,

> Everyone knew they had a place, and everyone stayed there. Some who were privileged used their position to help other blacks where they could. But for the most part, those who had the advantage were just glad to be who they were.

Phyllis, who attended Dunbar and Howard in the 1940s, agreed that "Dunbar had a reputation of favoring light people." It was commonly acknowledged that "if you were light, but were not too bright [smart], you would be able to get by." Iva referred to this as a "way being made for you."

How common was social flight from Dunbar for reasons relating to complexion? Since the options for District students were limited, movement was not widespread. However, the number of Dunbar students who knew of "social transfers" all attributed this action to complexion and class politics. In 1952 one black mother, who lived in a housing project in Washington after relocating from North Carolina, recorded her thoughts on her child's education in the District:

"The school's all right, but nobody likes the principal."

"Why?"

"Oh, she calls the parents names and pushes the children around. She calls 'em stupid an' dumb an' all kinds of names. She's colored herself, but she's light-complected [sic]. She calls the students black. She's got no right to do that."[7]

Melvenia, a 1950 Dunbar graduate, exhibited no uncertainty when discussing a close friend's transfer from Dunbar: "Lighter people were privileged at Dunbar. [A friend] felt discriminated against and left." Milton, a friend of Melvenia's, concurred: "Color was a big issue in D.C. Both of my brothers were light. They went to Dunbar. I consider myself to be brown." Milton was the only of his siblings to attend Armstrong High School, the "less selective" institution.

The social pressure associated with selecting a high school in Washington was powerful enough and pervasive enough that many dark-skinned Washingtonians, prior to 1954, claimed that they tended to gravitate to Armstrong, the technical high school directly across the street from Dunbar. "There was never any choice with Dunbar; either you were going to be a professional, or you were going to be an auto mechanic," said Ross. "If you were going to be a professional, you went to Dunbar." A 1951 Dunbar graduate observed,

> If you went to Dunbar, you were either very smart or very light. If I am a low C student and I am very light, the rules would be bent. If you were dark with tremendous potential, you would be an asset to the school. It may have been that way by design . . . but usually if you were a very fair black person it was a presupposition that you went to Dunbar. Most of the dark-skinned people did tend to [go to] the technical high school.

The belief in de facto segregation at Dunbar High was an active agent in the decision-making processes of students. "If you feel you are not supposed to be somewhere and you're not wanted," said Otis, a dark-skinned University of Maryland administrator, "you go elsewhere. We all heard the stories about what we were supposed to be. Light, bright, and near white. We weren't that. So we left." He recalled that his mother's decisions about his schooling were based solely on complexion.

Once the impact of *Brown v. Board of Education* (1954) was felt throughout the city, floods of lower-class and darker-complexioned blacks made their way from Armstrong High to Dunbar; at the same time, Dunbar students moved into white schools. According to Taunya, an attorney in Baltimore, "[1958] was [the] year that Dunbar graduated its last 'elite' class. Teachers were beginning to push students into mixed schools, [but] color was still a big issue."

"There are some old Dunbarites who still reminisce about the good old days before things changed," said Ross. "Many older Dunbar alumni will always hang onto their memories of when things were different, more separate and, in their eyes, better."

Dunbar was well known for offering the student body "formal" entrance into adult society through a debutante ball sponsored by Bachelor-Benedict, a social organization of black men who had as one of their primary objectives the formal introduction of young black women into society. Bachelor-Benedict started in New York in 1921 and has hosted chapters in most major cities, organizing at least one major cotillion per chapter each year.

In Washington, the debutante ball provided a platform for the children of "society" Washingtonians to re-create adult soirées. It was among the most popular District events through the mid-1900s and was well attended by Dunbar alumni, Howard faculty and staff, and well-known citizens of the District. During the 1940s, forty to fifty women would be involved as debutantes, one former debutante recalled. About half the women were from Dunbar, but a young woman might be asked to join if she or her parents were associated with the organizers of the event. At that time, the cost was covered by whoever sponsored the young lady to be involved. Once the young woman secured a sponsor, she attended several dress rehearsals. It was also necessary to have an escort in black tie. The event was often held in the Lincoln-Colonnade Ballroom in Washington, the place, according to one interviewee, a native Washingtonian, "where the big bands came and [young folks] would throw big parties." In other years, it would be held at the Whitelaw Hotel.

One Dunbar graduate named Sewell remembered when the Bachelor-Benedict planning committee would meet at his uncle's farm, located in a Washington suburb. He said,

> They would all come up there, all of the people involved in Bachelor-Benedict, and they would eat and drink and laugh. And in between—of course—they would try to get some work done.

From the late 1950s to the present, the event has been restricted to twenty or thirty women. While the number of people attending the event increased, the number of selected women decreased. With these changes, the expenses of being a Bachelor-Benedict debutante have increased, but admittance to the event, according to my interviewees, has become more open to those who want to attend without participating.

Dunbar Alumni at Howard University

Many Dunbarites attended Howard University after high school, distinguishing themselves by their position as native Washingtonians. According to a 1955 Howard alumnus, "Dunbar black people thought they were the smartest black people who ever walked the face of the earth!" Non-Washingtonians at Howard quickly gained a "certain perception" about the old boys' network among the elite Dunbar crowd. According to this alumnus,

> It is part of the perception that I have gained over the years—not just at Howard, but as I've seen what's happened to those folks from Dunbar, particularly as they infiltrated and rose at the university—they were all, every one, fair.

For Dunbar graduates, Howard was a natural extension of high school. Most of the Dunbarites at Howard, according to a Dunbar-Howard alumnus, "tended to stick together on Howard's campus" and often "had an air about us [when] among the other students."

Dr. Arthur, another 1955 Howard graduate and now a neurologist practicing in Baltimore, felt that Dunbar was in fact a micro-Howard, "in quite the same was that Howard was a macro-Dunbar." As the children of deans, professors, and university administrators, many of the younger generation of "Old Washington" inhabitants held a claim to the university and viewed nonnatives as "visitors to the temple." Dr. Arthur said that they "truly felt that Howard was entirely their university, since it was in the nation's capital where they resided. Also, living off-campus gave them an air [of distinction]. They probably did what most people would do if you were in their hometown; they felt a bit superior and different."

The Dunbar-Washington clique at Howard was often called the "Black Intelligentsia" on campus because, according to Dr. Daniel, one of Dr. Arthur's classmates:

If you weren't from D.C., you couldn't get into their group. Even if you were a rocket scientist. They were old-line, very fair-skinned people. And no matter how much money you had, you couldn't be part of them.

Organizations and cliques on campus were re-creations of local cultures and communities in a university setting. Dr. Daniel continued,

The kids from New York, Philadelphia, and Newark were working class. But a lot of the kids from D.C. and the South were really aristocrats. They came from professional families. They were second and third generation in college. And a lot of them looked on the northern kids as thugs!

This doctor, who entered Howard in 1951, went despite warnings that he would be "socially unsuccessful" because of his dark complexion.

One 1946 Howard graduate, George, who was a premed student, aptly noted that the cliquishness among Dunbar graduates was only "natural," and rather than a consequence of discriminatory intent, their closed coterie was the obvious repercussion of attending an internationally celebrated college in their hometown. Also, considering the unique quality of black life in Washington—"[T]he students from Washington tended to be more sophisticated. They had been exposed to much more, and many were from professional families," George concluded—the inherent dissimilarity with other blacks could be interpreted and misinterpreted in any number of ways.

The History of Color Prejudice at Howard

Howard University was founded in 1866 by O. O. Howard, a white United States Army general. Incorporated in 1867, the private school received most of its early support from the Bureau of Refugees, Freedmen, and Abandoned Lands, an annual subsidy of $10,000. By 1930 the school received almost $1.5 million in support.[8] With this financial endowment, Howard developed ten programs of study—including a school of music, a school of religion, and a college of medicine—which provided more options for concentrated instruction than most historically black colleges.[9]

Color prejudice at Howard—or the belief in color prejudice—was a topic of discussion even during the very early history of the school, as an 1887 scandal involving the medical school valedictorian illustrates. At Howard's medical school, a two-thirds-majority vote was required for one to be elected as valedictorian. White students, who were small in number at Howard, nominated C. C. Johnson, a fair-complexioned man who "[could not] be distinguished from white." The black students protested his selection, indicating that he was too light to represent the experience of black students; white and fair students protested the counter-selection of a dark student for similar reasons. The issue was referred to the faculty, who selected a young woman as valedictorian. She identified herself as white.[10]

During this time, Washington, D.C., was still a predominantly southern city, and Howard was part of a consortium of southern, historically black colleges that contended with rumors of colorism in its admission practices and staffing policies. Fair-skinned blacks in the administration were often perceived at Howard to give preferential treatment to "those who resembled themselves"; moreover, they were thought to exercise a monopoly over black higher education.[11] There were also said to be many instances throughout Howard's history of faculty members who blurred the race line—passing for white while maintaining full association with the historically black college—an indication of the level of invisibility of black life to their white contemporaries.

In 1914, fifty-seven black institutions were listed in *The Negro Year Book* under "Universities and Colleges"; twenty-six of the thirty-one black presidents of these schools were identified as mulatto. Of the remaining five, three were black and two failed to record their racial origin. "Howard University," said one Washingtonian who attended the University of the District of Columbia, "was thought of as a very snobbish school. My high school was across the street, and we even had our prom at Howard. We knew that it had a reputation of catering to very fair people."

At this time, one district resident stated that the "talented tenth and socialites of Howard University dominated Washington society" and struggled tirelessly to maintain exclusive ties and a high-toned appearance.[12] In the same way that Washington was a conglomeration of cultures, so, too, Howard University became a repository for local practices, practices that young blacks had learned in their cities and towns and now had a chance to practice on their own.

By 1940, 46 percent of all black doctors, 40 percent of all black dentists, and 46 percent of all black lawyers came from Howard. Moreover, 49 percent of all African Americans holding master's degrees gained them from Howard's graduate programs.[13]

In 1927 writer Langston Hughes took note of the complexion consciousness that existed at many black institutions, not the least of which was Howard, and declared it nothing short of alarming: "Speaking of a college fraternity dance, one in a group of five college men said, 'there was nothing but pinks there,—looked just like fay [white] women.'" He also noted that fair women were not above acknowledging dark classmates with only the "coolest of nods."[14] Zora Neale Hurston, a friend of Hughes's and a fellow Harlem Renaissance writer, had attended Howard and described it in similar terms:

> Now as everyone knows, Howard University is the capstone of Negro education in the world. There gather Negro money, beauty and prestige. They say the same thing about a Howard man that they do about Harvard—You can tell a Howard man as far as you can see him, but you can't tell him much. He listens to the doings of other Negro schools and their graduates with bored tolerance. Not only is the scholastic rating at Howard high, but tea is poured in the manner![15]

While the practice of paper bag testing at Howard is believed to have dissipated after the 1960s, the rumors of the test's existence persisted. In fact, a member of Howard University Law School's class of 1986, Mrs. Williams, remembers a "paper bag party" thrown by fellow classmates during the year of her graduation. According to her,

> A guy who was the son of [a prominent university official] was one of the main ringleaders. He was part of the organizing. It was my last year. They were talking about having a party and they wanted to do something different. And someone said, "We should have a paper bag party. Most of us could come." And I said, "Surely, you're kidding." And it probably took a week or two to die down, and before people took seriously that it was going to happen. They were initially very serious about having it.

As an explanatory note, or as further evidence of this occurrence, she described the nature of the group hosting the party. Because this informant heard about this party firsthand, it would certainly not qualify as a legend but, instead, as the transposition of a legendary tradition into a practiced tradition. Mrs. Williams acknowledged this, saying,

In one sense, they may have been mocking the tradition. But I also think they were going to be telling people, "You shouldn't be here if you don't meet the criteria." And they would have excluded them as they have been excluded in the past.

Another informant, Maxine, recalled how she had applied to Howard in 1958, hoping to fulfill her dream of attending this renowned "capstone of Negro education"—a dream that was shared, incidentally, by her large, supportive family. After being informed of her acceptance, her first thought was of how she would return home in a year like other students from Houston, Texas, who had gone to Howard: a "race hero," a novelty, a chosen member of the elite Howard family.

Maxine joined the Howard-Houston Club, "a local [Houston-based] group that would introduce incoming students to Howard students in the area." While these people quickly became big brothers and sisters to younger students, she said, "they also introduced me to 'color tests' and other elitist practices at Howard." Maxine's vision of Howard and notions of the power and import of the "black elite" became distorted before she had even set foot on the university campus.

During her junior year at Howard, Maxine roomed with a friend who was "dark, had short hair, and—on top of that—she didn't have good grades and wasn't from an influential family." Maxine remembered that the girl would "wear a scarf around the nape of her neck all of the time," which was so uncomfortable that she would "twist her head around all day." Once, when Maxine asked her why she wore it, the student responded, "It makes me feel like I have long hair."

"No matter how close we were, she still had a feeling that she didn't fit in with us because her hair was different," said Maxine, a tall, fair-skinned woman with large bright eyes and scattered freckles. "This was typical of the mood and the type of environment that the university fostered." According to Dr. Daniel, who had attended Howard seven years earlier,

> It was sometimes a socially cruel environment, and if you were not considered to be attractive, you were isolated. For the most part, if you were dark, you were not accepted at Howard. The common feeling was if you weren't considered attractive, you could stay in your room for a long time without going out.

At Howard, according to Maxine, "you could not be on a court unless you were very fair," and the women selected as queens were "always the whitest of the fair women on campus." Maxine, who was chosen for the Alpha court, the Omega court, and the ROTC court, remembered,

> The Kappas [Kappa Alpha Psi fraternity] would pick the lightest girls on campus and say, "We have to match [her with] our colors; red and white!" The Alphas [Alpha Phi Alpha fraternity] would try to pick a golden tone to match their colors [black and gold]! They all gave some reason, but they all chose fair-skinned, long-haired women as queens.

Dr. Daniel, who pledged Alpha Phi Alpha in 1951, agreed that "the selection process was very rigorous. Somebody would put a name up [and] people would discuss this person. Then we would vote on it." It was not uncommon for members to rule out a candidate, stating that the candidate was "too dark to be on our court." "Too dark" generally referred to virtually any shade of brown. In 1952 younger members of Alpha at Howard bloc-voted for a brown-skinned girl from Florida to be the court queen. "As far as I know, Pat was the brownest queen Alpha ever had at Howard," said Daniel. Pat later married the son of Howard president Mordecai Johnson.

Another informant, Dr. Arnold (a friend of Dr. Daniel's), stated,

> To us, Mordecai Johnson was quite a hero. We put him on the same level as Benjamin Mays, who was at the forefront of black educators. I think, as an institution, students at Howard felt they were at the Mecca of black education.
>
> We didn't put much credence into it at the time, but Mordecai Johnson was a light-complexioned black from Virginia. And, incidentally, Mordecai's son married a dark-skinned woman. We all noticed that!

In 1960 a brown-skinned woman lobbied to win homecoming queen. As an academically unsuccessful student, she was denied a bid, based on the 2.5-grade-point-average requirement. "It was a real grassroots operation," recounted Maxine, who cites this instance as the first evidence of social resistance during her time at Howard. Although the woman was not permitted to run, she gained unprecedented popularity and admiration among her classmates.

The Admission Picture Test

Through the early part of the twentieth century, it was customary to send a picture along with one's application to Howard. The common legend was that a prospective student's skin tone was "evaluated" and was a key factor in whether or not one would be accepted.[16] A Baltimore doctor who entered Howard in 1952, Dr. Arnold heard legends concerning the purpose of the admission picture:

> At the time it was pretty well known the usual [intraracial] prejudices existed [at Howard]. It was the story during our time that—for young ladies, anyway—you had to send a picture to Howard, but it would be hard to confirm what the reason was. This is something I heard before I came to the university; I heard that colorism was a factor in sending the picture, and it had a big impact on your admittance to Howard.

The admission picture custom was often used to poke fun at dark-complexioned Howard students. A very fair-complexioned member of the class of 1960 (a classmate of Maxine's) recalled being stopped while walking across campus with a dark-skinned friend; the friend was asked, "Did you forget to send your picture?" The question, by that time, implied that the person being addressed was out of place. My informant continued,

> There was nothing we could say, because we all knew what it meant. As far as they were concerned, she was not suitable to be at Howard because of her color.

Well into the 1960s, stories about the admission picture test were still circulated outside the university, although it had lost some of its steam on campus. A graduate of Morgan State who applied to college in 1965 said that he "did not even consider sending an application to Howard, because I had heard that I would have to send a picture, and that dark people were treated unfairly both in the admission process and on campus." This informant, who went on to become a successful musician and storyteller, said that the Howard legacy of discrimination was well circulated in his northern Maryland neighborhood and that, although most of his friends went on to college, none considered Howard among their choices.

Avon Dennis, Howard University's director of admissions, confirmed that a picture was once required for admission; the purpose of the picture was to identify students once they arrived on campus. But he does not quickly dismiss the possibility of a more calculated agenda. He stated, "I'm very familiar with that legacy, and I cannot say that there is no truth to it. I know that you still, to this day, hear a lot about the admission picture and complexion on campus." Even so, Dennis contended that while "we have all heard the rumors, and some folks believe them . . . it is doubtful that complexion played any role in the development of this institution."[17]

The "admission picture" still stands as one of the most active caste legends at the university. "If they didn't use a picture to determine tone," one member of the class of 1940 observed, "then how was it that when I got there almost everyone happened to look near white, like me?"

Sororities on Howard University's Campus

In 1908 a group of women who were enrolled at Howard University decided, under the guidance of fellow student Ethel Hedgeman, to form a sorority. Hedgeman borrowed the idea from her boyfriend (and future husband), who had joined a black fraternity, Alpha Phi Alpha, started two years earlier at Cornell University. Along with eight other women, she started Alpha Kappa Alpha at Howard University. In the beginning, the group "had no academic grade requirement, no charter or constitution and congregated for social relief from the rigors of university study."[18] The women who started AKA were of a variety of hues and backgrounds: Hedgeman was born in 1885 of humble beginnings. Another founder was the first graduate of Baltimore Colored High School to attend Howard. Yet another was the child of sharecroppers.

In 1912 several AKA members became disenchanted with the "artistic" nature of the group. They decided to dissolve AKA and form a new organization aimed at "meeting the challenges of the changing times." This new organization, formed by twenty-two former AKAs, was called Delta Sigma Theta. Delta became known as the first community-service black sorority.[19] A few women remained loyal to the original AKA group and regenerated it in later years, adding an initiation ceremony, a constitution, and increasingly rigorous academic requirements.

Seven years after Delta was founded, a third sorority, Zeta Phi Beta, was formed to serve as the sister organization to the newly chartered Phi Beta

Sigma fraternity. The two groups became the first black fraternity and sorority bound by constitution, and the sorority was the first black sorority for which members were selected primarily on the basis of academic achievement.

It is certainly the perception—and sorority photographs in Howard yearbooks suggest it—that through the 1930s, '40s, and '50s the women who were selected for Zeta were generally darker than the women who were selected for AKA and significantly darker than members of Delta Sigma Theta. (Although AKA is most often charged with complexion-based discrimination, Delta women are historically—and, based on the photographic evidence, undeniably—the fairest-hued women at Howard.) In my interview with Zeta founder Myrtle Tyler Faithful, she informed me, "We weren't looking at how rich you were or what you looked like or how you dressed." Instead, according to Faithful, Zeta developed a reputation for selecting a greater variety of women, who were interested in pursuing the ideals of "academic excellence, finer womanhood, sisterly love, and Christian values." Zeta has been perceived, throughout the sororities' history, as less selective. Generally, chapters of any black sorority that includes a large number of darker members are labeled "less selective," with complexion being a clear and present marker of selectivity. One Zeta, who attended Howard in the 1940s, recounted a formal Greek affair on Howard's campus where, "among a room of fifty to one hundred Greeks, the darkest one would usually be the Zeta, the sole colored girl among all of those black people."

At Howard, with the Zetas and Sigma Gamma Rho (the fourth black sorority established) exempt from charges of colorism, the AKAs and Deltas contended with each other and with issues of intraracial racism. The majority of the legends of "tests" in Howard's black organizations have been associated with these sororities' admissions practices. According to one AKA, a native of Tennessee who pledged at Howard in the late 1930s,

If you were too dark . . . you weren't going to be considered to make line. There was no need for any kind of test. You just weren't considered, no questions asked, and no explanation given.[20]

Evelyn, the daughter of well-to-do Tennessee natives, pledged AKA at Howard in 1945. "There were about one hundred AKAs on campus when I became involved and there were maybe thirty on our line," she said. At that time, according to Evelyn, few women would seek membership: "Usually we were asked to join." Evelyn—who was dubbed "little white Evelyn" by her high school teachers—did not gain a sense of her "social privilege" until she came to Washington, D.C. "Everybody wanted me," she recalled. "I got rushed by everybody. I had a friend who looked like me and she was rushed into everything too." She and her friend were initially interested in Delta, "which had more of a mixture," but eventually the two decided to pledge the high-toned Alpha Kappa Alpha.

Evelyn remembered that a good-spirited intimidation was involved in the pledging process. "We really enjoyed it!" she said. (This was well before the 1980s, when the extreme pledging practices of some black fraternities and sororities drew significant news coverage.) Women who were recruited by the AKAs would be invited to join the "Ivy Leaf Club," AKA's interest group. "Ivys" were required to wear their hair in two pigtails and paint their faces pink and green (the sorority colors). "We just did it to be ridiculous; we were just having fun," Evelyn recalled.

Official membership requirements for AKA included a respectable grade point average (over 2.5), activity in the campus community, and, according to Evelyn, "exhibition of finer womanhood." In less formal terms, an individual had to be well liked by the group in order to join, and how well one was liked might be influenced by a number of social and superficial factors.

Evelyn acknowledged that members of her sorority often commented on the complexion of an applicant when considering them for membership:

> I've heard sisters [in AKA] say things about dark girls, and I didn't appreciate it. They would talk about how they look, how they sound. I felt that these were human beings, and who are we to say they aren't good enough?

Colorism played a role in Evelyn's decision not to be active with the sorority after graduation. "That's just the way the system worked," she continued. "Often I don't even think about discrimination because there was nothing really to argue about. It's just the way it was."

In 1951 Dr. Daniel—then a freshman—was told that both the AKAs and the Deltas practiced the paper bag test:

I heard they used to put a brown paper bag up against the wall, and if you came in the room and you put your hand against that bag and you were darker than the bag, you weren't accepted. I heard that for both the Deltas and the AKAs.

Although Daniel does not remember where he first heard about the test, he noted that—after seeing the fair-skinned women the two sororities (particularly the Deltas) selected—"one would have to assume that it was true." Very little was said about the other sororities on campus, according to Daniel.

Ethele, a retired social work professor at Howard who had pledged AKA as a student at Temple University, heard similar stories when she joined the Howard faculty. "I heard that all the fair girls went Delta and the brown girls went AKA. All of the dark girls would go Zeta." Ethele, who was a close friend of AKA founder Ethele Hedgeman Lyles, claimed that she had not heard about the sorority practicing a "paper bag test" but that elitism in sororities was very much the norm at Howard University. Ethele continued,

[These clubs] were a matter of your family being old-line Washington: There are the "What Good Are We." I've heard that it's a closed social group that has been meeting for the last fifty years. The Hellians. These are old-line Washingtonians. This is what is interesting about black folk: Going to college and getting your education is one thing. But it's a matter of the family [background].

The "paper bag" legend remained relatively unchanged, although small variations from different time periods were reported. Some indicate that the bag was placed against the face of the applicant. Others suggest that the aspirant had his or her hand placed inside the bag. Still others say that the bag was held against the wall and that the student would be asked to stand beside it. Maxine attended Howard less than ten years after Daniel, and the legend she heard went like this: "The brown bag test was where you would hold a brown bag up to your face, and if you were darker than the paper bag, you couldn't get into certain groups."

The woman who relayed this story to Maxine was, Maxine claimed, subjected to the test. In the end, the woman was not accepted to pledge either the AKAs or the Deltas. She was one of two women Maxine knew personally who claimed to have been subjected to the test. Maxine recalled conversations at Howard-Houston Club meetings:

> They used to talk about the paper bag test and the flashlight test as a way of getting into a Greek organization, and I thought it was funny. It was hurtful only because it was a dark-skinned person telling me the story who could not pass any of the tests. And we were all sitting down at a meeting, and we were just joking about it until I found out what it really meant. She had actually been subjected to the test and hadn't passed.

A second woman recounted an experience identical to Maxine's. "She was [also] dark, with very short hair," Maxine remembered. However, she gained membership to the group in 1962. "I was told that was the year the organizations did away with the test. I was told that if it was a year earlier, she wouldn't have gotten in. That's just to show you how far these organizations had come [by] 1962."

The circulation of stories about paper bag tests in black sororities was one of the primary methods of maintaining the elite membership that these organizations sought. Students were often told about these legends upon entering the university, which discouraged some women from seeking memberships. Other tests associated with sororities at Howard included blue vein tests and flashlight tests. Mack, a resident of Philadelphia, recalled a cousin who claimed she was subjected to a "vein test" while attempting to pledge a sorority at Howard in the 1940s:

> If a girl's veins didn't show in her legs—which meant she was light-skinned—then she wasn't welcomed to join this particular sorority. She had actually tried to join, which one it was, I can't now remember. From time to time she would talk about it as she got older.

Dr. Arnold discussed the requirements imposed on those being considered for fraternity queen at Homecoming, in this case for his fraternity, Omega Psi Phi:

> The fraternities were looking for a nice-looking black female. Of course at that time, black meant everything except black *hue*. It meant if a female didn't have the "super curley" [Afro] hair and who had features more related to the basically identified black person. Even the dark, dark people were still superior [for] being at Howard. It's like, "I'm the dog in the king's house,

but I'm still in the king's house." If you went to Shaw University, for example, then you were the king *in* the doghouse.

Yet another test with a rumored history at Howard was the flashlight test, which maintained association with both the AKAs and the Deltas until 1958. A 1964 Howard graduate explained this test:

> In the flashlight test, they'd have you stand in profile and shine a flashlight on your face and they would look at the shadow that was cast. And if your mouth or your jaw extended beyond your nose, you could not pass.

There were, according to many 1950s and 1960s Howard students, three ways to get around the tests. "If your parents knew people, if you have a lot of money, or if you had a dynamic academic average and they needed your [grades]," Dr. Daniel said. Another alumni, a member of the class of 1957, agreed that "it wasn't always [a question of] color." In many cases, "it was how well your family was known" and respected.

Francis, the daughter of a Delta Sigma Theta cofounder, suggested that many legends may be a "veil" used by unpopular students attempting to "pass the blame" for their social isolation:

> If I don't get into a sorority, then I am going to look around for a reason, and color may sometimes be a convenient excuse. They say "it's my color," or "they don't like me," or any excuse to try and figure out why you're not accepted by this group of women. As I look at [Delta chapters], I'd say color is not an issue.

Herself a Delta and a member of the Links, Inc., Francis said, "There are evil women everywhere, so I can't say it didn't happen." Also, she added, members sometimes "set up their own rules in their minds, feeling that if the organization is too open, it's no longer an honor that they want." Francis, who grew up in Maryland, often heard stories about colorism outside the sorority from her mother, a native Washingtonian:

> I've been reading a lot of [my mother's] speeches recently. She was coming out of Washington. She would say that none of these [Washington] people have any class. And when we asked her why, she said all they think about is color. And this struck us. My mother told us that the reason there were color issues was because people couldn't make it on any other level. Therefore,

people would stratify and create differences. Certainly there were some clubs in D.C. that felt if you didn't pass the color of—whatever it was—you couldn't come in. But that has never affected me one bit.

It was important to me to investigate the relationship between sorority membership and complexion, since this seemed to be yet another "site" where written histories could be amended through a reading of color politics.

Zeta Phi Beta cofounder Myrtle Tyler Faithful stated in 1991 that "color certainly played a significant role in your placement at Howard University." Some embrace the idea that Zeta was founded as a refuge for darker women at Howard. Faithful stated simply,

> Every group tries to define themselves differently. Zeta was founded as a sister organization to Phi Beta Sigma Fraternity. That was part of our founding.

She then added hesitantly,

> But we also saw that there were certain women—certain Howard women— who had social needs on campus, and that those needs were not met by any of the existing groups.

Writer Zora Neale Hurston, who pledged Zeta Phi Beta while a student at Howard, confirms this. She attended the high school department of Morgan College (now Morgan State University) in Baltimore, where many of the wealthy, beautiful, and fair-skinned children prepared to enter Howard. "I had heard all about the swank fraternities and sororities and the clothes and everything and I knew I could never make it," she recalled.[21] However, after arriving at Howard, Hurston joined the Zeta Phi Beta sorority and took part in "all the literary activities on the campus." She thus identified a community that could embrace her.[22]

In *Don't Play in the Sun*, her 2004 memoir of growing up dark brown in Washington, D.C., writer Marita Golden recalls receiving affirmations of complexion consciousness from Howard administrators. One told her,

> I remember hearing people say awfully cruel things about Zetas. They were called the black and ugly sorority because most of their members were brown-skinned or dark-skinned.[23]

The idea of complexion discrimination and the discussion of tests were "frightening and hurtful," said Maxine. In the end, they were successful in their objective: they dissuaded dark-skinned women from attempting to join organizations. In fact, the legend may have been intimidating enough—that is, the idea was as forceful as the application. In any case, the 1960s brought a needed wind of change to the sorority movement. "It went all the way over to the other side," one 1962 student activist stated, "and it became ugly to be light." Instead of sororities instantly gaining a greater mix, pledging became "uncool," and the darker majority rallied against the social cliques that had divided the black community for years. Sororities experienced an all-time low in new membership, and in keeping with the times, they attempted to reshape their agendas to conform with the national mood.

Against this wind of change, isolated incidents of colorism were still witnessed at the university. In 1985, as I noted earlier in this study, select members of Howard University's graduating law class hosted a paper bag party. Although Greek life was less influential among Howard's graduate community, Mrs. Williams, the informant who told me this story, said that many Greeks were part of a distinguishable clique known as the "beautiful people." She identified these students as

the ones who have a very light complexion. They had select parties and only certain people could go. And it was always a question of who your daddy was, and if you were the "blue blood" of this area or that area.

Mrs. Williams—a Zeta, the daughter of an influential Maryland family, and a graduate of Vassar College—was chastised by classmates for not selecting Alpha Kappa Alpha or Delta Sigma Theta, but she did not regret her choice to stay far from the groups that were "always caught up in competing for who was the prettiest." She said,

It was amazing to me—all of the little situations I saw while at Howard. What you look like would get you to a certain point. Then, who you were might take you a little further.

Another informant, Maxine, noted that, when put in context, "Greek organizations reflect the attitudes of people in larger society," where "we still prefer people with light skin. People with long flowing hair. People with fine features." She added, "Even if fraternities and sororities don't have 'tests' anymore, people are still using [complexion] as a marker."

Q.T., who started graduate school at Howard in 1967, recalled that "change had really begun to take place" when he arrived on campus. A year earlier, Robin Gregory had become the first homecoming queen with an Afro hairstyle. According to Q.T.,

> There was a group of students who had been put out for demonstrating. There were standing court cases against the university to get them back in. There was a growing number—or a core of student activists—who wanted to bring black consciousness to the campus. A lot of students had been directly involved in civil rights, and these students set the mood for changing attitudes about class and color.

The mood at Howard echoed the mood of the country, and slowly but surely the students were turning around the psychology of an institution, a city, and a nation.

Chapter 6

Complexion and Worship

> I heard people talking about the M—— Church, and
> they say that it is a "dicty" church. They have even said
> that the church is made up of people who are light in
> complexion . . . I think the people talk that way simply
> because the church has a sermon of "common sense" and
> there is no shouting and tearing of the benches.
>
> **Vattel Elbert Daniel**
> **"Negro Classes and Life in the Church"**

If we accept the role of the black church as the center of black life, then the
arrangement of black churches ought to reflect, confirm, and affirm the arrangements that exist in the community. In *The Philadelphia Negro*, W. E. B.
Du Bois wrote that "the Negro church came before the Negro home" and
that "it stands . . . as the fullest, broadest expression of organized Negro life."
He continued,

> The Negro church is not simply an organism for the propagation of reli-
> gion; it is the centre of social, intellectual and religious life of an organized

group of individuals.... [T]he church has been peculiarly successful so that of the 10,000 Philadelphia Negroes whom I asked, "Where do you get your amusement?" fully three-quarters could only answer, "From the churches."[1]

Before the 1830s, all people of color in the District, enslaved or free, were forbidden to assemble for religious purposes without the attendance of a white clergyman. This was the source of significant moral and social objection among blacks—some white pastors even refused to hold black babies in their hands during the rite of baptism—and the desire to form separate houses of worship intensified. Among the early black churches in the District were Mount Moriah African Methodist Episcopal (A.M.E.), founded in 1816, and Metropolitan A.M.E. (1822), the church attended by Frederick Douglass. Most established blacks in the city sought affiliation with Methodist churches, the denomination that had become synonymous with middle-class status in white America and among the established black classes. In fact, in terms of the parishioners they hosted, black churches were a tidy replication of church hierarchy as it existed among whites: for example, from the 1820s until the 1860s, while white Methodist congregations were flooded with aristocratic slave owners, white Baptist churches were filled with laborers and were commonly believed to be less inclined towards pretension.[2]

The earliest black church to incorporate a social program within its religious agenda was Union Bethel African Methodist Episcopal Church, a house of worship located on L Street, Northwest. The Bethel Literary Society, a reading and discussion club for lettered black Washingtonians attracted, in the words of one historian, "the most intellectual men to lectures, to participate in discussions and read dissertations on timely subjects."[3] Implicit in the structure of this club was the expectation that membership seekers were schooled, a standard that, in practice, excluded the majority of black Washingtonians.

The Bethel Literary Society was thought to be a blue vein society that, unlike the "Old Cit" clubs, intended to include distinguished newcomers in the Washington social scene. The membership included many respected black Washington doctors, lawyers, and businessmen, as well as diplomats, scholars, and professionals visiting from other cities. But according to the *Washington Bee,* it was also a "cast [*sic*] organization ... on the order of the

Lotus Club," which discouraged the inclusion of messengers, domestics, and laborers.[4]

In design, in structure, and probably even in reality, the Bethel Literary Society was not an organization that practiced colorism—though it was selective. The weekly meetings, held on Monday evenings, would include music, song, essay reading, and addresses from distinguished persons. The membership consisted of many men and women who were not members of Bethel A.M.E. Church, but the presidency was assumed by the designated bishop of the A.M.E. Church. (While the rule of the bishop was accepted in the role of spiritual leader, his intellectual prowess could certainly be challenged by outsiders.)[5]

St. Luke's Protestant Episcopal Church—founded by Alexander Crummell in 1873—was attended by "established" residents in the city. The church was located on Fifteenth Street, Northwest, and on any given Sunday, one would find the most well-dressed men and women of mixed ancestry there sitting side by side with white men and women.[6] In fact, what distinguished St. Luke's from the elite black churches was the number of local whites who attended. Still, along with St. Mark's in Charleston, St. Thomas's in Philadelphia, and St. Phillip's in New York, St. Luke's was considered to be one of the most elite "black" churches in the nation.[7]

Similarly, the Nineteenth Street Baptist Church was labeled a "silk stocking" house of worship throughout the early twentieth century. First organized by four white ministers in 1802, Nineteenth Street was the first official Baptist congregation in the city and served a predominantly white membership. With an increasing number of blacks joining the congregation in the 1830s—including both freed persons and slaves—the whites opted to move out. In 1833 the edifice was sold to black Baptists. Nineteenth Street Baptist Church is now considered the "Mother church" of six Baptist congregations in Washington, D.C.[8]

This oldest Baptist congregation quickly became the "property" of the oldest citizens, many of whom were freed slaves. Before long, those women who could afford silk stockings were considered to be the more desirable Sunday worshipers, or so some thought. Unlike most of the other Baptist congregations, erected in quick succession, Nineteenth Street was called the "high-toned temple of worship" that "bore little resemblance to lower-class

Baptist congregations scattered throughout the rural south or poor districts of cities."[9] According to one native Washingtonian named Melvina,

> It was commonly known that the Nineteenth Street Baptist Church was the first to have a comb test. A deacon would stand at the door, and if your hair was too nappy, the deacons would actually ask you to worship elsewhere! Now I don't know anyone who actually experienced it. But you can ask anyone who is familiar with that congregation and their traditions, and they will tell you.

This legendary test is the one most commonly associated with elite black churches, from Catholic churches in New Orleans, where it is believed to have originated, to Christian Methodist Episcopal churches in Ohio. This legend suggests that a comb was hung, usually on a hook by a front door, and was used to test the hair texture of potential congregants. If the person's hair snagged in the comb, they were not welcome to worship. In Philadelphia, it was believed that one Episcopal church in particular was reserved "for the people who were very fair." A native Philadelphian said,

> In the [early days] most folks who belonged to the Episcopal church were very fair. And they were—as they say—"good haired" people. They were the elite—you know—of the bourgeoisie class. Now dark skin people . . . might have been made to feel unwelcome.

The religious politics of Philadelphia echoed the problems facing Washington. An 1887 editorial in the *Washington Bee* stated,

> There is a certain class of colored people in the [Washington] community who carry their prejudice in the church [and] the pulpit. . . . We know cases to have existed where members were *too black for the congregation.*[10]

It was the perception of this tradition, along with fear of public humiliation, that prevented some black Baptists in Washington from seeking membership at Nineteenth Street. The historically poignant question is what actual traditions of Nineteenth Street Baptist allowed such a negative association to emerge and survive several generations. As with most rumors, the lore about Nineteenth Street responded to the unanswered questions of the majority who did not attend Sunday service there. The church, because of its age, prominence, legacy, and history, attracted many middle-class and some wealthy members, many of whom, by social and class design, were more fair in complexion. Also, while the black church as a collective body functioned as the hub of black communities, black communities were generally not privy to the social agendas of individual congregations.

The "clientele" of Nineteenth Street was decidedly different from the high aristocratic brotherhood of the Fifteenth Street Presbytery. The majority of the Nineteenth Street membership were removed from the Howard-Dunbar set, and while many maintained organizational affiliations with upscale groups, their social circles were not recognized by the "upper tens." Middle-class residents of the "Gold Coast," many of whom were fair but not card-carrying aristocrats, frequented Nineteenth Street Baptist. They were the lower-ranked elite: their homes were along Sixteenth Street, Northwest, and along Rhode Island Avenue; they sometimes adopted the values of neighboring white congregations but also originated their own methods of worship and fellowship.[11]

In addition to its reputation as a comb-testing church, Nineteenth Street Baptist was often called the "blue-vein prayer circle" of the city. From the late 1930s until the late 1940s, visitors to the Nineteenth Street Baptist Church may have subscribed to the traditional belief that the handshake that greeted them at the door was in fact an opportunity to look at the visitors' veins to determine if they were visible through their skin.

One of the practices that led to the belief in discrimination was the inclusion of Nineteenth Street Baptist under the category of "silk-stocking churches." Generally speaking, the church upheld a stricter dress code than other Baptist congregations, which certainly may have quietly discouraged poorer persons from attending. As one native Washingtonian stated, "Women were expected to have silk stockings and gloves to worship there. And pearls and patent leather shoes didn't hurt." With all of its pretensions, the Nineteenth Street Baptist Church ranked second in snobbery, elitism, and colorism to the Fifteenth Street Presbyterian, the preeminent "blue vein" church in the city.[12]

First located between I and K Streets, Northwest, the Fifteenth Street Presbyterian Church was considered the most "color struck" of the black congregations in Washington. It was founded in 1841 by Reverend John Cook, a dark-complexioned minister with stewardship over a small but committed group of black Washingtonians. Born a slave and freed during his childhood, Cook grew up in Washington's small free black community. In 1817 his family opened the first school for blacks living in the city, and by 1834 he was named headmaster. He was licensed to preach in 1841, and the Fifteenth Street Presbyterian Church was founded the same year.[13] It was flooded by black Washingtonians who were, like Cook, freed tradesmen and business owners, many with elementary levels of education. Though subtle, the churches' tradition of elitism started here: Cook was black, but most of the freed people of color were mulattoes, and they flocked to his church, tired of filling the balconies of white Presbyterian churches. Cook's descendants, as noted earlier, went on to become the most elite, fair-hued, and aristocratic of the District 400s. At the Fifteenth Street Church, freed blacks continued the traditions of white Presbyterian churches, which—even from the early 1800s—catered to a "selective membership."[14]

By the late 1800s, Fifteenth Street had the reputation of being an elitist church where mulattoes formed the majority. Society columns commented on the shift in membership, claiming that the edifice had been "seized by strangers" and suggesting that this elitism was not caused by native Washingtonians but, rather, by recent migrants, who were mixed-race people from Louisiana's traditional three-caste system and southern mulattoes. In Louisiana these mixed-race people had been associated with the more conservative churches, mainly the Catholic Church, and had been schooled separately from freed blacks in the period immediately following emancipation. Small pockets of Louisiana natives in the District repeated this pattern of self-segregation. It was hardly coincidental that the Presbyterian Church is close in worship style to the Catholic Church and that many of these Louisiana Catholics flocked to it.[15]

Consistent with the congregation's perception of itself, the second pastor, Henry Highland Garnet, was a man of prominent standing in Washington, and during his pastorate he became the first African American to deliver a sermon before the United States House of Representatives. With the election of this new pastor, Washingtonians gossiped about what his appearance would be and whether the congregation would seize the opportunity to select a leader that favored, in complexion and social standing, the majority of the congregants.[16] On the dawn of Garnet's election, the *Washington Bee* asserted that the people of Washington would call the congregants to task if they continued to make a social mockery of God's house.[17] But the initiation of the pastor had begun, and so had the legacy of Fifteenth Street leadership by men who could distinguish themselves, even among aristocrats.

Members of Fifteenth Street in the early 1900s included Elizabeth Keckley, the seamstress to Mrs. Abraham Lincoln and, eventually, the financial caretaker of an impoverished Mary Todd Lincoln during the latter half of Mrs. Lincoln's life. When white historians of the day claimed that no such figure—one who supported an ailing white woman and gained such prestige among her own race and others—existed in the life of Mrs. Lincoln or otherwise, Francis Grimke, who served as Keckley's pastor at Fifteenth Street and officiated in her funeral, publicly vouched for her existence and for her membership at Fifteenth Street. "She used to come up the aisle," wrote Grimke, "the very personification of grace and dignity, as she moved towards her pew." Of her fair skin, delicate features, and stately appearance, Grimke said, "no one who ever saw her, or had any contact with her, even casually, would ever be likely to forget her."[18] Keckley was one of the most active members and generous contributors to the Fifteenth Street Church during her life.

Any given Sunday morning at Fifteenth Street brought together a who's who of Washington's black elite. As writer Julian Ralph described it,

> The [Fifteenth Street] Presbyterian Church is known as the religious rendezvous of the educated set and is necessarily small. The Rev. F. J. Grimke, a Negro and a Princeton graduate, is the Pastor. His flock is composed of school teachers, doctors, lawyers, dentists . . . no darky peculiarities in that edifice.[19]

The Bruces and the Wormleys, both names that were synonymous with "arrival" in society-Washington, were regular congregants. "It was like the underground railroad," according to one interviewee, a church official. He suggested that, just as you were likely to attend Fifteenth Street if you were part of high society, "you [often] had to come through Fifteenth Street to be part of high society." Richard T. Greener, a black Harvard graduate and classmate of Pastor Grimke, noted in a letter to Grimke that no other black church in the country "boast[s] a brighter array of talent, a more refined cultural auditory or that has more competent . . . public spirited pastors . . . than the Fifteenth St. Presbyterian Church in Washington, D.C."[20]

Until the 1950s, Fifteenth Street experienced little variation in its conservative worship style, which could be described as a precise mimicry of white Presbyterian churches. Sacred music and quiet worship helped members to live out the "Presbyterian proverb": "We do things decently." In the late 1950s, however, Fifteenth Street ushers were no longer attired in bow ties and tails during services; still, in practice and appearance, the church remained indistinguishable from white Presbyterian congregations.

A third-generation native Washingtonian, now a schoolteacher in Reston, Virginia, suggested that the set-up of the Fifteenth Street Church was like that of white churches where dark parishioners, the few who joined, worshiped from segregated galleries. He said,

> I can't say this is entirely true, but what was a fact was that the Fifteenth Street Presbyterian Church didn't welcome dark people. I heard that you had to be lighter than the [beige] color of the front door to get in. And then, after they started accepting darker people, they had to sit in the back, and lighter people sat in the front.

Folklore about the Fifteenth Street Church claims that it was the only Washington church to have a "door test." As an extension of this legend, most black Baptist churches—thought to be less refined in worship style and serving a darker-hued majority—painted their doors dark brown, while Presbyterians—catering to the well-born and light-toned—preferred a shade of tan or red. Whether or not there is any truth to these legends—and in some cases supporting evidence can be found—the stories provide a foreground for considering this history. For many people, it is the black church that is responsible for confirming discrimination, and similarly, the earliest complexion legends hail from religious institutions. Taunya, a Baltimore law professor and native of Washington, recalled hearing that the Fifteenth Street Presbyterian Church was a "paper bag church." But, she stated, "it was not an exclusion, it was a preference." One current leader of Fifteenth Street did not quickly dismiss this possibility, stating,

> I've heard that they had a paper bag test here and at Howard. I think there is truth in all of it. I believe it could have happened here. It's never been on the books, but it is real.

A Fifteenth Street Church official refers to this phenomenon as part of a "pit bull mentality":

> Everyone wants to protect their space. Traditionally, there exists a system of insiders and outsiders in some congregations.

A Xavier University archivist suggested that "complexion tests, if they occurred, would have peaked around the 1890s" and that they took on a legendary quality after the turn of the century. Nevertheless, given the reality of these religious congregations—that most of their regular members were fair-complexioned—the belief in such practices is not unfounded. The historical certainty is that Fifteenth Street remained elitist because it was part of a network, an infrastructure of elitism and discrimination. Dunbar High School, founded in the basement of Fifteenth Street, was recognized as the most elite black high school in the country. Dunbar faculty were often trained at Howard, and many attended Fifteenth Street Presbyterian. Many members of Fifteenth Street were also involved with Dunbar and Howard as benefactors, active alumni, advisors, or parents of Dunbar students. An official of Fifteenth Street said, "In this church we were trained this way . . . [to] build an infrastructure." In this infrastructure lay the origins of the Washingtonian aristocratic "underground railroad."

The perpetuation of church complexion legends speaks to the strict social arrangement of blacks within this small city's religious culture. The cases of Fifteenth Street Presbyterian Church, the Nineteenth Street Baptist Church, and, to a lesser degree, Union Bethel A.M.E. beg the question: has the black church in Washington fallen victim to the social trends reflected in the lore of black residents? The answer lies in the origin of the most long-standing legend—the paper bag test—and its history in the predominantly Creole

Catholic churches in Louisiana. Legends suggest that the very earliest acts of intraracial testing were among priests and Creole Catholics who chose a paper bag as a measure of "too dark." Some churches have consistently served to perpetuate discriminatory traditions. The power of the church lies in the arrangement of black leadership as well.

Finally, given the social, political, and economic importance of the black church, each church body grew to reflect the social, political, and economic agendas of its membership. The churches of the elite represented their interests, and maintaining a fair-toned membership was a significant part of how community "interests" were defined.

Chapter 7

One Drop of Black Blood, a Conclusion

> I have seen Washington, of which city I had heard much, and
> I have looked at something called "society" of which I had
> heard much too. Now I can live in Harlem where people are
> not quite so ostentatiously proud of themselves, and where
> one's family background is not of such great concern. Now I
> can live contentedly in Harlem.
>
> **Langston Hughes**
> **"Our Wonderful Society: Washington"**

In the introduction to the second edition of her book *Black Macho and the Myth of the Superwoman,* Michele Wallace wrote that after rereading her book, which deals with cultural myths about black American men and women, she wanted to destroy it because her desire for something more from life— more "than my marginal status as a black woman writer could ever offer"— was so palpable in the book's pages: "In obsessively repeating the stereotypes of black women and men, I wanted to burst free of them forever."[1] By "them," I am certain that she meant the thick stereotypes of blackness and gender. But I am also sure that she wished to break free from the need to write such a book at all. And I know how she felt. What would Wallace suggest to me, a young black woman early and vulnerable in her career, offering, as my first critical study of black life, the documentation of taboo material? I have struggled with this concern throughout this study.

In 1898 folklorist Fletcher Bassett described folklore as the "demonstrator of the possible and probable in history, the repository of historical truths otherwise lost, the preserver of the literature of the people, and the touchstone of many of the sciences."[2] Writer Marita Golden says it equally well:

> Writing about the color complex [in 2004] means thinking about the color complex, and the process becomes akin to breaking through a dense, evil encryption that masks, hides, denies, and silences the truth about what we have inflicted on ourselves. Writing this book, I inevitably seek out and find others brave enough to witness, question, and remember.[3]

While folklore is defined as the way that people craft their own stories, oral history involves the crafting of someone else's story by threading together various patches and pieces of information. While folklore is the compilation of "community material," oral history is the collecting and documenting of the product—determining how and why traditions grow and change. Through the union of oral history, we are able to flesh out motives, understand beliefs, and comprehend convictions: as such, we "democratize" history in a way that "History" cannot.

I have intentionally reserved this statement for the end of this study because I believe that this project has been a collaborative and participatory project to construct an addendum to the rich body of work being done on the black elite, the city of Washington, and color consciousness, as well as work done in African American folklife and folk traditions. What is the historical question being raised here? Generally, it is about whether it is possible to coordinate people's lived experience with history, and specifically, whether belief systems are the primary subtext of history, written through legend, ritual, customs, and traditions.

In returning to Michele Wallace's concern, I leave this project feeling with great conviction that "negative inquiry" is a phase of the celebration of culture. Many years ago, a colleague at an oral history conference described such inquiry as opening the heart of horrible things to see where they came from. It is my conclusion, then, that of the intraracial dilemmas facing African Americans, the least explored, but most prevalent, is the impact of complexion on social treatment and social experience. While many works by African American historians and social scientists have peripherally explored colorism, my first chapter makes evident that there exists no collective body of work or easy method of collecting this scattered material. In effect, material exists quantitatively, but virtually no qualitative attention has been given to folkloric material related to complexion. While literature in particular and black writing in general have not specifically supported the belief in formal intraracial discrimination, it has, with tremendous consistency, demonstrated that we blacks, among ourselves, have fully embraced the tradition of assigning social prestige based on hue. Newspaper editorials and social columns have, throughout history, celebrated the physical attributes of the fair hues; there is no shortage of photographic evidence that lighter skin, traditionally, matters. Complexion tests simply existed to give form to such beliefs.

It became evident over the course of this study that the language, the tone, and the words that Washingtonians used to tell their stories also capture the difficulty, the complexity, and the importance of determining what "blackness" has come to mean intraracially in a nation that has violated any potential to consider race, and thus color, without judgment.

Still, what end is advanced by devoting an entire work to colorism? First, it reinforces a simple truth in black life: that our practices, rituals, and beliefs are formed within the residual effects of racism. Second, it documents the existence of legends and of lore that have been part of the belief system of black communities. If we acknowledge that complexion superiority has been a de facto modus operandi in black communities, we must also acknowledge that it is a problem that requires continued examination.

As a folklore project, I view *The Paper Bag Principle* as a test case in the difficulty of collecting taboo material, in investigating practices that are visibly invisible—unspoken but heard—and in convincing people to retell stories that evoke fear and shame. I often found myself questioning the sustainability of a project based on material that is both speculative and certain, imagined and real, mythical and factual. In the end, while this study could be interpreted as a malicious exposé of black institutions' imperfections, it is, instead, a revisionist look at one predominantly black city that attempts to privilege belief and tradition in post-emancipation, New Negro, civil rights, Black Power, and urban cultural dynamics. It is through the study of these beliefs that we can construct a more discerning analysis of black community identity. It is an occasion to look at color—look at it closely—and conclude that within our collective success, there must be space for old conversations to be made new.

As Gwendolyn Brooks has noted, the "one drop of black blood" rule imposed by white America has made black America infinitely large. It at once disrupts strict definitions of race and confirms the benefit of being less "racial" in appearance. Though it was not my intent, I have come away with an awareness that at various points in history fairer-hued Washingtonians have, as a collective subculture, contributed to the compromised social status of some darker blacks in ways that paralleled white American racism; that the impact was mostly social differentiates it. In defense of this collective group, it can be said that the "mood of the time" dictates the behavior of the culture and that social conformity propels human behavior more than individual conviction. The phrase "it's just what we do" reverberates throughout and serves as the most active agent in this study. And, in this regard, the fair-toned black elite have been equally victimized by an unattainable Western ideal.

Black life histories subtly disclose the texture of black life and the complexities of upscale organizations, institutions, and communities. These groups and the people who constitute them struggle with self-definition, with success by American standards, and with physical proximity to the dominant society's vision of beauty. In his prophetic turn-of-the-century social study *The Philadelphia Negro,* W. E. B. Du Bois wrote,

> [T]his class, which ought to lead, refuses to head any race movement on the plea that thus they draw the very color line against which they protest. On the other hand their ability to stand apart, refusing on the one hand all responsibility for the masses of the Negroes and on the other hand seeking no recognition from the outside world, which is not willingly accorded—their opportunity to take such a stand is hindered by their small economic resources.... On the other hand, their position as the richest of their race—though their riches are insignificant compared with their white neighbors—makes unusual social demands upon them.[4]

Considering this as the broader social context crowds out the original objective, so far as the basic recording of complexion tests is concerned. The greater issue brought to light is the traditional influence of privilege and hue in shaping attitudes, race agendas, and race spokesmanship.

Even if the rules of intracultural interaction change, the social problem of intraracial lore will persist because it is driven by more fundamental American social-structural questions—questions whose answers are beyond the governance of black community, questions that will force the problem of intraracial social distinction to replicate itself in varying ways, even without the force of the will of the community sustaining it. Again, Marita Golden:

> In the 1950s I grew up in a largely segregated world. The only White people I came into contact with were teachers at school and a few fellow students in Washington D.C.'s even then majority Black school system. So I rarely heard words directly from the lips of Whites, addressed to me, or to other Blacks that assessed our relative beauty. But Whites had created another, ongoing, invasive and seductive and powerful conversation about beauty and color through movies and television and magazines and books and the collective imagination. And the language of that conversation was not only an echo of the self-hating dialogue among Blacks about skin color but also its progenitor.[5]

Social change has taken place, along with, but arguably not driven by, the acceptance of a select group of iconoclastic dark-skinned women as beauty symbols. The structure persists—the problems are important—but we must look at black life with an awareness that our culture is both worth preserving and worth changing. Inasmuch as it is changeable, it is, in fact, ever changing.

The legends that have circulated in Washington, D.C., help us to understand the preoccupations of African American urbanites in American city centers.

The settings change; the questions remain the same.

Notes

Introduction

1. Patricia A. Turner, *I Heard It Through the Grapevine: Rumor in African-American Culture* (Berkeley: Univ. of California Press, 1993), 5.

2. Willard Gatewood, *Aristocrats of Color: The Black Elite, 1880–1920* (Bloomington: Indiana Univ. Press, 1990), 7.

3. Lawrence Otis Graham, *Our Kind of People: Inside America's Black Upper Class* (New York: HarperCollins, 1999), 11.

4. Randall Kennedy, *Nigger: The Strange Career of a Troublesome Word* (New York: Pantheon Books, 2002), 4.

5. Ibid., 45–46. The folk verse that Kennedy quotes appears in Daryl Cumber Dance, *Shuckin' and Jivin': Folklore from Contemporary Black Americans* (Bloomington: Indiana Univ. Press, 1978), 77.

1. Traditions and Complexion Lore

1. Transcribed from a performance by Ivie Anderson and Duke Ellington, in *The Norton Anthology of African American Literature*, 2nd ed., ed. Henry Louis Gates Jr. and Nellie Y. McKay (New York: W. W. Norton, 2004), 66–67.

2. See Charles L. Perdue Jr., Thomas E. Barden, and Robert K. Phillips, eds., *Weevils in the Wheat: Interviews with Virginia Ex-Slaves* (Charlottesville: Univ. Press of Virginia, 1976), 232–33. Story provided by Levi Polland, a former slave.

3. Joseph E. Holloway, ed., *Africanisms in American Culture* (Bloomington: Indiana Univ. Press, 1990), 213.

4. J. Mason Brewer, *American Negro Folklore* (Chicago: Quadrangle Books, 1968), 20.

5. Zora Neale Hurston, *Dust Tracks on a Road: An Autobiography* (1942; reprint, New York: HarperCollins, 1995), 50–51.

6. Siobhan B. Somerville, *Queering the Color Line: Race and the Invention of Homosexuality in American Culture* (Durham, NC: Duke Univ. Press, 2000), 77.

7. Edward Byron Reuter, *The Mulatto in the United States: Including a Study of the Role of Mixed-Blood Races Throughout the World* (Boston: R. G. Badger, 1918), 19.

8. Ibid., 287.

9. Werner Sollors, *Neither Black nor White yet Both: Thematic Explorations of Interracial Literature* (1997; reprint, Cambridge, MA: Harvard Univ. Press, 1999), 127.

10. Mary V. Dearborn, *Pocahontas's Daughters: Ethnicity and Gender in American Culture* (New York: Oxford Univ. Press, 1986), 139–40.

11. From Claude McKay's poem "The Mulatto." See McKay, *Complete Poems* (Urbana: Univ. of Illinois Press, 2004), 210; originally published in *Bookman,* Sept. 1925.

12. T. S. Stribling, *Birthright* (New York: Century, 1922), 203.

13. Ibid., 98.

14. Nella Larsen, *Quicksand* and *Passing,* ed. Deborah E. McDowell (New Brunswick, NJ: Rutgers Univ. Press), 203. This reprint edition in Rutgers's American Women Writers Series includes the complete texts of both novels. The quotation is from *Passing.*

15. Sterling Brown, *The Negro in American Fiction* (1937; reprint, New York: Arno Press, 1969), 144–45.

16. Dion Boucicault, *The Octoroon; or, Life in Louisiana* (1851; reprint, Miami: Mnemosyne Publishing, 1969), 17.

17. I use "she" and "her" as universal pronouns, but, fittingly, it is rare that authors dedicate a full work to the life dilemmas of quadroon males.

18. Joseph Holt Ingraham, *The Quadroone; or St. Michael's Day* (1841; reprint, Kessinger Publishing, 2004), 5.

19. See Charles Parrish, "Color Names and Color Notions," *The Journal of Negro Education* 15 (1946): 13–20. This article was derived from chapter 3 of Parrish's 1944 doctoral dissertation, "The Significance of Color in the Negro Community," at the University of Chicago.

20. Ray B. Browne, *Popular Beliefs and Practices from Alabama* (Berkeley: Univ. of California Press, 1958), 10.

21. Chrisena Coleman, *Mama Knows Best: African-American Wives' Tales, Myths, and Remedies for Mothers and Mothers-to-Be* (New York: Simon & Schuster, 1997), 65.

22. Ntozake Shange, *for colored girls who have considered suicide when the rainbow is enuf* (New York: Macmillan, 1989), 56.

23. Madame C. J. Walker is credited with distribution of the straightening comb in 1905. While the hot comb only changes the texture of black hair temporarily, it is still a well-used method of hair dressing for younger black women, as well as an alternative to hair relaxers, which permanently alter hair texture. Walker is remembered as the first black woman millionaire in the history of the United States. See Nowliwe Rooks, *Hair Raising: Beauty, Culture, and African American Women* (New Brunswick, NJ: Rutgers Univ. Press, 1996), 51–52.

24. Ruth Benedict, *Patterns of Culture* (Boston: Houghton Mifflin, 1934), 13.

25. See George C. Wolfe, *The Colored Museum* (New York: Broadway Play Publishers, 1988), 19.

26. Gwendolyn Brooks, "Hattie Scott: at the hairdresser's," in *The World of Gwendolyn Brooks* (New York: Harper and Row, 1971), 37.

27. Browne, *Popular Beliefs and Practices,* 126.

28. Assata Shakur, *Assata: An Autobiography* (Westport, CT: Lawrence Hill and Co., 1987), 31.

29. Browne, *Popular Beliefs and Practices,* 52

30. From an advertisement that appeared in *Half-Century* magazine in the 1950s.

31. From an advertisement for Nadinola skin bleacher that appeared in the Washington-based *Afro American* in 1950.

32. Wallace Thurman, *The Blacker the Berry: A Novel of Negro Life* (1929; reprinted with an introduction by Therman B. O'Daniel, New York: Collier Books, 1970), 125.

33. Rudolph Fisher, "High Yaller," *Crisis* 30–31 (Oct. 1925): 282.

34. Sw. Anand Prahlad, *African American Proverbs in Context* (Jackson: Univ. Press of Mississippi, 1996), 106–7.

35. In his introduction to Wallace Thurman's *The Blacker the Berry,* Therman B. O'Daniel comments on the popularity of this saying in black life, and the irony it introduces, since black complexion is more often "the source of sorrow, humiliation, and pain." It might even be read as a satire that critiques the black preoccupation with skin color by altogether reversing a stereotype. See Thurman, *The Blacker the Berry,* ix.

36. Hurston, *Dust Tracks on a Road,* 184.

37. From "Lay Ten Dollahs Down," in *Encyclopedia of Black Folklore and Humor,* ed. Henry D. Spalding (Middle Village, NY: Jonathan David Publishers, 1972), 245.

38. Shakur, *Assata,* 30.

39. From "Yellow Girl Blues," in *Blues Lyric Poetry: An Anthology* (New York: Garland Press, 1983), ed. Michael Taft, 4.

40. Thurman, *The Blacker the Berry,* 179

41. From "Black Gal Swing," in Taft, *Blues Lyric Poetry,* 37.

42. See Howard Odum and Guy Johnson, *The Negro and His Songs: A Study of Typical Negro Songs in the South* (Chapel Hill: Univ. of North Carolina Press, 1925), 187.

43. From "Tight Haired Mama Blues," in Taft, *Blues Lyric Poetry,* 160.

44. Kobena Mercer, "Black Hair/Style Politics," *New Formations* 3 (1987): 34.

45. Ibid., 51–53.

46. From "You Can't Win, Gentlemen!" in Spalding, *Encyclopedia of Black Folklore,* 315.

47. Dance, *Shuckin' and Jivin',* 77.

2. A National Perspective on Complexion Lore

1. See George S. Schuyler, "Who is 'Negro'? Who is 'Black'?" *Common Ground* 1 (Autumn 1940): 54; and Adrian Piper, "Passing for White, Passing for Black," *Transition: An International Review,* no. 58 (1992): 4–32.

2. Claude McKay, *A Long Way from Home* (1937; reprint, New York: Arno Press, 1969), 110–11.

3. Larsen, *Passing,* 150.

4. Gertrude Atherton, *Senator North* (New York: John Lane, 1900), 94–95.

5. Frances Parkinson Keyes, *Crescent Carnival* (New York: Franklin Watts, 1942), 253.

6. Schuyler, "Who is 'Negro'? Who is 'Black'?" 55.

7. Dorothy Canfield, *The Bent Twig* (New York: Henry Holt, 1915), 72.

8. Schuyler, "Who is 'Negro'? Who is 'White'?" 55.

9. Constance McLaughlin Green, *The Secret City: A History of Race Relations in the Nation's Capital* (Princeton, NJ: Princeton Univ. Press, 1967), 207–8.

10. Piper, "Passing for White, Passing for Black," 7.

11. Ibid., 9

12. Eli S. Marks, "Skin Color Judgements of Negro College Students," *Journal of Abnormal Psychology* 38 (July 1943): 370–76.

13. Parrish, "Color Names and Color Notions."

14. Marks, "Skin Color Judgements," 375.

15. Graham, *Our Kind of People,* 17.

16. Ibid.

17. Henry Louis Gates Jr. and Cornel West, *The Future of the Race* (New York: Alfred A. Knopf, 1996), 18.

18. Anna Lee West Stahl, "The Free Negro in Ante-Bellum Louisiana," *Louisiana Historical Quarterly* 25 (1942): 310–12.

19. Arna Bontemps, "The Invisible Migration," in *They Seek a City* (Garden City: Doubleday, 1945), 99.

20. W. E. B. Du Bois, *The Philadelphia Negro: A Social Study* (1899; reprinted with a new introduction by Elijah Anderson, Philadelphia: Univ. of Pennsylvania Press, 1996), 204.

21. See Gatewood, *Aristocrats of Color,* and Vattel Elbert Daniel, "Negro Classes and Life in the Church," *Journal of Negro Education* 13 (Winter 1944): 19–29.

22. Mark Mathabane, *Kaffir Boy in America: An Encounter with Apartheid* (New York: Charles Scribner's Sons, 1989), 24–25.

3. Washington Society

1. Langston Hughes, "Our Wonderful Society: Washington," *Opportunity* 5, no. 8 (Aug. 1927): 226.

2. Ibid.

3. Paul Laurence Dunbar, "Negro Life in Washington," *Harper's Weekly,* Jan. 13, 1900, 32

4. Hughes, "Our Wonderful Society," 227.

5. William Henry Jones, *The Housing of Negroes in Washington, D.C.* (Washington, D.C.: Howard Univ. Press, 1929), 47.

6. See Mary Mitchell, *Chronicles of Georgetown Life: 1865–1900* (Cabin John, MD: Seven Locks Press, 1986), 90–94.

7. Mary Elizabeth Corrigan, "A Social Union of Heart and Effort: The African American Family in the District of Columbia on the Eve of Emancipation" (PhD diss., Univ. of Maryland, College Park, 1996), 4.

8. Dunbar, "Negro Life in Washington," 9, 18.

9. Booker T. Washington, *Up From Slavery* (1901; reprint, Signet Classics, 1969), 59.

10. Mary Church Terrell, "Society among the Colored People of Washington," *Voice of the Negro* 1 (Mar. 1904): 152–53.

11. Hal Chase, "William C. Chase and the *Washington Bee*," *Negro History Bulletin* 36 (Dec. 1973): 172–73.

12. Corrigan, "A Social Union," 4–6; A. H. Shannon, *The Negro in Washington: A Study in Race Amalgamation* (New York: W. Neale, 1930), 35.

13. Ronald M. Johnson, "From Romantic Suburb to Racial Enclave: LeDroit Park, Washington, D.C., 1880–1920," *Phylon* 45, no. 4 (Dec. 1984): 268–70.

14. Ibid., 266.

15. Mary Church Terrell, *A Colored Woman in a White World* (1940; reprint, New York: G. K. Hall, 1996), 113.

16. Johnson, "From Romantic Suburb to Racial Enclave," 264–67.

17. Paul Laurence Dunbar, "Negro Society in Washington," *Saturday Evening Post,* Dec. 14, 1901, 9.

18. Johnson, "From Romantic Suburb to Racial Enclave," 269.

19. Jean Strouse, "The Unknown J. P. Morgan, "*New Yorker,* Mar. 29, 1999, 65–79.

20. Jacqueline Moore, "One Drop of African Blood" (PhD diss., Univ. of Maryland, 1994), 15–16.

21. George B. Hutchison, "Jean Toomer and the 'New Negroes' of Washington," *American Literature* 63, no. 4 (1991): 686.

22. Ibid., 683–86.

23. Jean Toomer to Claude McKay, Aug. 19, 1922. Quoted in Charles Larson, *Invisible Darkness: Jean Toomer and Nella Larsen* (Iowa City: Univ. of Iowa Press, 1993), 16.

24. Ibid., 17.

25. Jean Toomer, "Withered Skin of Berries," in *Wayward Seeking: A Collection of Writings by Jean Toomer,* ed. Darwin T. Turner (Washington, D.C.: Howard Univ. Press, 1980), 139–65.

26. Hutchinson, "Jean Toomer and the 'New Negroes' of Washington," 686.

27. Terrell, "Society among the Colored People of Washington," 151–52.

28. Gatewood, *Aristocrats of Color,* 58.

29. Ibid., 44.

30. Hughes, "Our Wonderful Society," 226–27.

31. This last statement is meant to be a charge against white society, still unwilling to embrace near-white black aristocrats. It could be read as a veiled charge against the black women aristocrats and their separatist agenda. See "Negroes of Rank: Racial Diversion of the Colored Aristocracy of Washington, Caste Prejudice Still Exists," *Spectator* (1890). Clipping in Cook Family Papers, Moorland-Spingarn Research Center, Howard University.

32. Gatewood, *Aristocrats of Color,* 40.

33. See letter from Francis Grimke to G. Smith Wormley (grandson of James Wormley), in "Communications," *Journal of Negro History* 21, no. 1 (Jan. 1936): 57–58.

34. Moore, "One Drop of African Blood," 14.

35. Editorial, *Washington Bee,* July 24, 1886.

36. Gatewood, *Aristocrats of Color,* 56, 59.

37. Hughes, "Our Wonderful Society," 226.

38. Gatewood, *Aristocrats of Color,* 46.

39. Constance McLaughlin Green, *Washington,* vol. 2, *Capital City, 1879–1950* (Princeton, NJ: Princeton Univ. Press, 1967), 110.

40. Hughes, "Our Wonderful Society," 226.

41. "The Colored Social Settlement," unpublished study, Francis Grimke Papers, Moorland-Spingarn Research Center, Howard University.

42. Ibid.

43. Terrell, "Society among the Colored People of Washington," 152.

44. Mary Church Terrell, "Why, How, When and Where Black Becomes White," unpublished essay, Mary Church Terrell Papers, Moorland-Spingarn Research Center, Howard University, Washington, D.C., n.p.

45. Ibid.

46. Green, *The Secret City,* 207–8.

47. Nannie Helen Burroughs, "Brotherhood and Democracy," radio broadcast transcript, Feb. 27, 1938, Frederick Douglass Papers, Moorland-Spingarn Research Center, Howard University, 2.

48. Stokley Carmichael and Charles Hamilton, *Black Power* (New York: Vintage Books, 1967), 44.

49. Parrish, "Color Names and Color Notions," 13–20.

50. Rayford Logan, "Growing Up in Washington: A Lucky Generation," lecture, Columbia Historical Society, Sept. 20, 1977, transcript in Rayford Logan Papers, Moorland-Spingarn Library, Howard University, Washington, D.C., 3–5.

4. Social Organization in Washington

1. Gatewood, *Aristocrats of Color,* 47–48.

2. Walter L. Fleming, *The Freedmen's Savings Bank: A Chapter in the Economic History of the Negro Race* (Chapel Hill: Univ. of North Carolina Press, 1927), 1, 15–16.

3. *Washington Bee,* Feb. 2, 1884.

4. Editorials, *Washington Bee,* Jan. 19, 1884; Jan. 2, 1880.

5. *Washington Bee,* Feb. 2–16, 1886.

6. *Washington Bee,* Nov. 17, 1883.

7. Ibid.

8. Throughout the middle of the next century, the Fifteenth Street Presbyterian Church was still considered a high-toned temple of worship.

9. Dunbar, "Negro Society in Washington," 9.

10. *Washington Bee,* Mar. 15, 1884.

11. *Washington Bee,* July 10, 1886.

12. Terrell, "Society among the Colored People of Washington," 156.

13. The black (most often mulatto) Cosmos Club shared its name with a white club of the same name that was founded earlier. After the Monocan Club disbanded, the white Cosmos Club was integrated, but not before black Washingtonians had "passed" into the club undetected. Black members included Rayford W. Logan, author of *Howard University: The First Hundred Years* (New York: New York Univ. Press, 1969). Some of Logan's letters (see Rayford Logan Papers, Moorland-Spingarn Research Center, Howard University) reference the Cosmos Club, including one dated January 11, 1981, and addressed to Phillip Highfill, then president of the club.

14. *Washington Bee,* Jan. 18, 1890.

15. *Washington Bee,* Feb. 21, 1905.

16. The organization argued that mulattoes should enjoy the same privileges as white citizens. This group was so exclusive that even dark-hued mulattoes were excluded from joining. See John E. Bruce, "Colored Society in Washington," undated typescript, John E. Bruce Family Papers, Moorland-Spingarn Research Center, Howard University.

17. Editorials, *Washington Bee,* Dec. 17, 1904; Feb. 11, 1905.

18. Quoted in Haynes Johnson, *Dusk at the Mountain: The Negro, the Nation, and the Capital; A Report on Problems and Progress* (Garden City: Doubleday, 1963), 171.

19. Shirlee Taylor Haizlip, *The Sweeter the Juice: A Family Memoir in Black and White* (New York: Simon & Schuster, 1994), 79.

20. *Washington Bee,* Dec. 29, 1883.

21. Quoted in Johnson, *Dusk at the Mountain,* 169.

22. Editorial, *Washington Bee,* July 3, 1886.

23. Editorial, *Washington Bee,* Dec. 17, 1904.

24. Terrell, "Society among the Colored People of Washington," 156.

25. Nannie Helen Burroughs, "Not Color but Character," *Voice of the Negro* 1 (June 1904): 277.

26. Sandra Fitzpatrick and Maria R. Goodwin, *The Guide to Black Washington: Places and Events of Historical Significance in the Nation's Capital* (New York: Hippocrene Books, 1990), 56.

27. Undated memo, MuSoLit Papers, Moorland-Spingarn Research Center, Howard University. See also Gatewood, *Aristocrats of Color*, 214.

28. *Washington Bee*, Apr. 27, 1918.

29. Ibid.

30. Booker T. Washington, N. B. Wood, and Fannie Barrier Williams, *A New Negro for a New Century* (Chicago: American Publishing House, 1900), 101.

31. See comments of Jack and Jill founder Louise Truitt Jackson Dench on the main page of Jack and Jill's Web site at http://www.jack-and-jill.org/.

32. Margaret Turner Stubbs Thomas, Jack and Jill Web site, main page.

33. Graham, *Our Kind of People*, 22

34. "A History of Jack and Jill," unpublished manuscript, Jack and Jill of America, Inc., New York Chapter, Records, Schomburg Center for Research in Black Culture, New York Public Library.

35. Graham, *Our Kind of People*, 31.

36. Ibid., 32.

37. "History of the Girl Friends," unpublished manuscript, Girl Friends, Inc., Records, Schomburg Center for Research in Black Culture, New York Public Library.

5. School Lore

1. E. Delorus Preston, "William Syphax, a Pioneer in Negro Education in the District of Columbia," *Journal of Negro History* 20, no. 4 (Oct. 1935): 458–59; Rayford Logan, "Middle-Class Black Washington Life," (lecture, Feb. 1, 1978, Rayford Logan Papers, Moorland-Spingarn Research Center, Howard University, Washington, D.C.).

2. "The Color Line in Our Public Schools" (1936), unpublished report, Mary Church Terrell Papers, Moorland-Spingarn Research Center, Howard University, Washington, D.C.

3. Preston, "William Syphax," 470.

4. "The Color Line in Our Public Schools."

5. Logan, "Middle-Class Black Washington Life."

6. See Dunbar, "Negro Society in Washington," 9, and Terrell, "Society among the Colored People of Washington," 152.

7. Quoted in Johnson, *Dusk at the Mountain,* 175.

8. "Clad in Robes of Majesty: Howard University is Capstone of Negro Education," *Brown American,* May 1940. Issues of this periodical were collected in several volumes by the Negro Universities Press, Westport, Connecticut (1970); see vol. 4 (1940–1941): 10–11.

9. Ibid., 11.

10. *Washington Bee,* Dec. 24, 1887.

11. Gatewood, *Aristocrats of Color,* 162.

12. Quoted in Gatewood, *Aristocrats of Color,* 68.

13. "Clad in Robes of Majesty," 11.

14. Hughes, "Our Wonderful Society," 226.

15. Hurston, *Dust Tracks on a Road,* 129.

16. After I looked at every available Howard University yearbook published over a seventy-year period (1908–78), it became quite obvious to me that there are periods during which claims of colorism in social organizations or in general admissions would be hard to prove. For example, from 1912 to 1928, most organizational photographs, as well as other Howard photos, seem to suggest a full integration of students of different hues. However, it is also obvious that a rather dramatic shift seems to have taken place in the selection of campus queens and social organization members around 1932 in favor of lighter women, a shift that was sustained until about 1952.

17. Avon Dennis, director of admissions at Howard, attended Morgan State University. He was interviewed on February 10, 1997.

18. Paula Giddings, *In Search of Sisterhood: Delta Sigma Theta and the Challenge of the Black Sorority Movement* (New York: William Morrow, 1988), 38.

19. Ibid., 45.

20. Traditionally, those pledging black fraternities and sororities had to maintain military-style formations during the process—thus, "making line" refers to one's being invited to pledge a particular Greek-letter society.

21. Hurston, *Dust Tracks on a Road,* 129.

22. Ibid., 138.

23. Marita Golden, *Don't Play in the Sun: One Woman's Journey Through the Color Complex* (New York: Doubleday, 2004), 46.

6. Complexion and Worship

1. Du Bois, *The Philadelphia Negro*, 469–70.

2. John W. Cromwell, "The First Negro Churches in the District of Columbia," *Journal of Negro History* 7, no. 1 (Jan. 1922): 64–65.

3. Ibid., 64–107.

4. *Washington Bee*, July 31, 1886.

5. *Washington Bee*, Dec. 23, 1882.

6. E. N. Chapin, *American Court Gossip, or Life at the National Capitol* (Marshaltown, IA: Chapin and Hartwell, 1887), 38.

7. Gatewood, *Aristocrats of Color*, 280–87.

8. Cromwell, "First Negro Churches," 76.

9. Haizlip, *The Sweeter the Juice*, 79.

10. *Washington Bee*, Dec. 17, 1887 (emphasis in original). Of course, fair-skinned blacks often felt that they, too, were the objects of prejudice and unfair stereotyping. Author Haynes Johnson recalled meeting a Howard student who "could have passed for a white man" and who was sometimes asked to authenticate legends about elitist black churches in his home town, Charleston, South Carolina. "They would ask me," he told Johnson, "if it's true that in my church the ones with the lightest skins sit on one side and the dark on the other. Of course it's not true. . . . [T]he light-skinned Negro catches it from both sides. He's almost like a middle group. He catches slander from both the whites and the darker blacks." See Johnson, *Dusk at the Mountain*, 174.

11. Cromwell, "The First Negro Churches," 80.

12. Gatewood, *Aristocrats of Color*, 274, 287.

13. Papers of the Fifteenth Street Presbyterian Church, Washington, D.C. This information was taken from the historical records of the church, provided by the current pastor, Reverend Sterling Morse.

14. Cromwell, "First Negro Churches," 80–81.

15. Ibid., 101–3.

16. "A History of the Fifteenth St. Presbyterian Church," undated, unpublished manuscript provided by Reverend Morse.

17. *Washington Bee*, Sept. 11, 1886.

18. Elizabeth Keckley's book, *Behind the Scenes* (New York: G. W. Carleton, 1868), details her relationship with Mary Todd Lincoln during the life of President Abraham Lincoln and the period following his assassination. Grimke's appraisal of Keckley appeared in "Communications," *Journal of Negro History* 21 (Jan. 1936): 56–57.

19. Julian Ralph, *Dixie; or, Southern Scenes and Sketches* (New York: Harper and Brothers, 1896), 368–69.

20. Quoted in Gatewood, *Aristocrats of Color,* 287.

7. One Drop of Black Blood

1. Michele Wallace, *Black Macho and the Myth of the Superwoman* (1979; reprinted with new introduction and bibliography, London: Verso Press, 1990), xxii–xxiii.

2. Quoted in Rosemary Zumwalt, *American Folklore Scholarship: A Dialogue of Dissent* (Bloomington: Indiana Univ. Press, 1988), 23.

3. Golden, *Don't Play in the Sun,* 53.

4. Du Bois, *The Philadelphia Negro,* 177–78.

5. Golden, *Don't Play in the Sun,* 9.

Bibliography

Special Collections and Family Papers

Moorland-Spingarn Research Center, Howard University, Washington, D.C.

Alpha Kappa Alpha Papers
Bethel Literary and Historical Association
John E. Bruce Family Papers
Roscoe Conklin Bruce, Sr., Papers
Anna Julia Cooper Papers
Mary Ann Shadd Cary Papers
Cook Family Papers
Cromwell Family Papers
Frederick Douglass Papers
Fifteenth Street Presbyterian Church Papers
Rayford Logan Papers
James Guy Tyson Papers
Mary Church Terrell Papers
MuSoLit Club Records

Schomburg Center for Research in Black Culture, New York Public Library

Ralph Bunche Papers
Girl Friends, Inc., Records
Langston Hughes Papers
Jack and Jill of America, Inc., New York Chapter, Records
Booker T. Washington Collection

Dissertations, Theses, and Unpublished Manuscripts

"The Colored Social Settlement." Francis Grimke Papers, Moorland-Spingarn Research Center, Howard University.

Burroughs, Nannie Helen. "Brotherhood and Democracy." Frederick Douglass Papers, Moorland-Spingarn Research Center, Howard University

Corrigan, Mary Elizabeth. "A Social Union of Heart and Effort: The African American Family in the District of Columbia on the Eve of Emancipation." PhD diss., University of Maryland, 1996.

Fry, Gladys Marie. "Activities of the Freedmen's Aid Society in the District of Columbia, 1860–1870." Master's thesis, Howard University, 1954.

Gass, Mercedia. "Blacks in Washington, D.C., 1800–1865." Master's thesis, Howard University, 1975.

Green, Horace. "Migration Patterns of the African Americans After Emancipation." Ralph Bunche Papers, Schomburg Center for Research in Black Culture, New York Public Library.

"History of Alpha Kappa Alpha Sorority as Given by Soror Beulah Burke on Founder's Day, February 16, 1941 at Howard University." Alpha Kappa Alpha Papers, Moorland-Spingarn Research Center, Howard University, Washington, D.C.

"History of the Fifteenth Street Presbyterian Church." Provided by Rev. Sterling A. Morse, pastor, Fifteenth Street Presbyterian Church, Washington, D.C.

Inter-racial Committee of the District of Columbia. "The Color Line in Our Public Schools." Mary Church Terrell Papers, Moorland-Spingarn Research Center, Howard University, Washington, D.C.

Logan, Rayford. "The Blackologist, the Blackoisie and the Big Lie." Rayford Logan Papers, Moorland-Spingarn Research Center, Howard University, Washington, D.C.

———. "Growing Up in Washington: A Lucky Generation." Rayford Logan Papers, Moorland-Spingarn Research Center, Howard University, Washington, D.C.

———. "Some Major Problems of Negroes in Washington, D.C., During World War I." Rayford Logan Papers, Moorland-Spingarn Research Center, Howard University, Washington, D.C.

Moore, Jacqueline. "A Drop of African Blood: The Washington Black Elite from 1880–1920." PhD diss., University of Maryland, College Park, 1994.

Parrish, Charles. "The Significance of Color in the Negro Community." PhD diss., University of Chicago, 1944. A condensed version of chapter 3 of this dissertation was published in the *Journal of Negro Education;* see next section.

Terrell, Mary Church. "What Colored Women Have Done in Clubs and Hope to Do." Mary Church Terrell Papers, Moorland-Spingarn Research Center, Howard University, Washington, D.C.

———. "Why, How, When and Where Black Becomes White." Mary Church Terrell Papers, Moorland-Spingarn Research Center, Howard University.

Winch, Julie Patricia. "The Leaders of Philadelphia's Black Community, 1787–1848." PhD diss., Bryn Mawr College, 1983.

Published Articles

Barnes, Annie. "The Black Beauty Parlor Complex in a Southern City." *Phylon* 36 (June 1975): 149–54.

Barras, Jonetta Rose. "Color Blind: How Melanin, Class and Culture Divide Black Washington." *Washington City Paper,* February 2, 1995.

Boas, Franz. "The Real Race Problem." *Crisis* 1 (1910): 22–25.

Bragg, George F. "The Episcopal Church and the Negro Race." *Historical Magazine of the Protestant Episcopal Church* 4 (March 1935): 47–52.

Burg, B. R. "The Rhetoric of Miscegenation: Thomas Jefferson, Sally Hemmings and Their Historians." *Phylon* 47, no. 2 (June 1986): 128–38.

Burgess-Ware, Louise. "Bernice the Octoroon." *Colored American Magazine,* August 1903, 607–61; September 1903, 652–57.

Burroughs, Nannie Helen. "Not Color but Character." *Voice of the Negro* 1 (June 1904): 277–79.

Chase, Hal. "William C. Chase and the *Washington Bee.*" *Negro History Bulletin* 36 (December 1973): 172–74.

"Clad in Robes of Majesty: Howard University Is Capstone of Negro Education." *Brown American,* May 1940.

"Class Distinctions Among American Negroes." *Southern Workman* 27 (October 1899): 371.

Clephane, W. C. "Local Aspects of Slavery in the District of Columbia." *Records of the Columbia Historical Society* 3 (1900): 237–56.

Cromwell, John W. "The First Negro Churches in The District of Columbia." *Journal of Negro History* 7, no. 1 (January 1922): 64–107.

Daniel, Vattel Elbert. "Negro Classes and Life in the Church." *Journal of Negro Education* 13 (Winter 1944): 19–29.

Davis, Madison. "The Navy Yard Section During the Life of the Rev. William Ryland." *Records of the Columbia Historical Society* 3, no. 20 (November 1900): 199–256.

Diedrich, Maria. "'My Love Is Black As Yours Is Fair': Premarital Love and Sexuality in the Antebellum Slave Narrative." *Phylon* 47, no. 3 (September 1986): 238–47.

Dunbar, Paul Laurence. "Negro Life in Washington." *Harper's Weekly,* January 13, 1900, 9, 32.

———. "Negro Society in Washington." *Saturday Evening Post,* December 14, 1901, 9, 18.

Durant, Thomas J. "The Black Middle Class in America: Historical and Contemporary Perspectives." *Phylon* 47, no. 4 (December 1986): 253–63.

Evans, Arthur S. "Pearl City: The Formation of a Black Community in the New South." *Phylon* 48, no. 2 (June 1987): 152–64.

Fisher, Rudolph. "High Yaller." *Crisis* 30–31 (October 1925): 281–86.

Fitchett, E. Horace. "Origin and Growth of the Free Negro Population of Charleston, South Carolina." *Journal of Negro History* 26, no 4 (October 1941): 421–37.

Foner, Laura. "Free People of Color in Louisiana and St. Dominique." *Journal of Social History* 3 (Summer 1970): 406–30.

"Frederick Douglass an Indian." *New Orleans Republican Courier,* January 20, 1900.

Freeman, Howard. "Color Gradation and Attitudes Among Middle-Income Negroes." *American Sociological Review* 31 (1966): 365–74.

Harris, Robert L., Jr. "Charleston's Free Afro-American Elite: The Brown Fellowship Society and the Humane Brotherhood." *South Carolina Historical Magazine* 82, no. 4 (October 1981): 289–310.

Hughes, Langston. "Our Wonderful Society: Washington." *Opportunity* 5, no. 8 (August 1927): 226–27.

Hutchison, George B. "Jean Toomer and the 'New Negroes' of Washington." *American Literature* 63, no. 4 (1991): 683–92.

Johnson, Ronald M. "From Romantic Suburb to Racial Enclave: LeDroit Park, Washington, D.C., 1880–1920." *Phylon* 45 (December 1984): 264–70.

Johnson, Toki Schalk. "Stunning Group of Socialites Take Part in Festivities." *Chatterbox,* May 1956.

Levey, Jane Freudel. "The Scurlock Studio." *Washington History* 1, no 1 (Spring 1989): 41–58.

Lewis, Vashti. "The Near-White Female in Frances Ellen Harper's *Iola Leroy.*" *Phylon* 45, no. 4 (December 1984): 314–22.

Love, Spencie. "Charles Drew and the Legend That Will Not Die." *Washington History* 4, no. 2 (Fall/Winter 1992–93): 5–19.

Marks, E. S. "Skin Color Judgments of Negro College Students." *Journal of Abnormal Psychology* 38 (July 1943): 370–76.

Mercer, Kobena. "Black Hair/Style Politics." *New Formations* 3 (1987): 33–54.

Milburn, Page. "The Emancipation of Slaves in the District of Columbia." *Records of the Columbia Historical Society* 16 (1913): 96–116.

"Negroes of High Rank." Newspaper clipping, circa 1890, publisher unknown. Cook Family Clippings, Moorland-Spingarn Research Center, Howard University.

Nelson, Henry Loomis. "The Washington Negro." *Harper's Weekly,* July 9, 1892, 654.

Ochillo, Yvonne. "The Race-Consciousness of Alain Locke." *Phylon* 47, no. 3 (September 1986): 173–81.

Parrish, Charles H. "Color Names and Color Notions." *Journal of Negro Education* 15 (1946): 13–20. This article was adapted from chapter 3 of Parrish's doctoral dissertation; see previous section.

Piper, Adrian. "Passing for White, Passing for Black." *Transition: An International Review,* no. 58 (1992): 4–32.

Pool, Maria Louise. "Told By An Octoroon." *Galaxy 10* (December 1870): 827–28.

Preston, E. Delorus, Jr. "William Syphax: A Pioneer in Negro Education in the District of Columbia." *Journal of Negro History* 20, no 4 (October 1935): 448–76.

Russell, John. "Colored Freemen as Slave Owners in Virginia." *Journal of Negro History* 1, no 3 (June 1916): 233–42.

Schmidt, Alvin J. "The Unbrotherly Brotherhood: Discrimination in Fraternal Orders." *Phylon* 34 (September 1973): 275–82.

Schuyler, George S. "Who is 'Negro'? Who is 'White'?" *Common Ground* 1 (Autumn 1940): 53–56.

Spalding, Henry D., ed. *Encyclopedia of Black Folklore and Humor.* Middle Village, N.Y.: Jonathan David Publishers, 1972.

Strouse, Jean. "The Unknown J. P. Morgan." *New Yorker,* March 29, 1999, 66–79.

Terrell, Mary Church. "Society among the Colored People of Washington." *Voice of the Negro* 1 (March 1904): 150–56.

Thompson, Richard W. "Phases of Washington Life." *Indianapolis Freeman,* June 8, 15, 1895.

Wesley, Charles H. "The Concept of Negro Inferiority in American Thought." *Journal of Negro History* 25, no 4 (October 1940): 540–60.

Williams, Fannie Barrier. "Perils of the White Negro." *Colored American Magazine.* Undated clipping. Moorland-Spingarn Research Center, Howard University.

Woodson, Carter G. "The First Negro Churches in the District of Columbia." *Journal of Negro History* 7, no. 1 (January 1922): 64–106.

Books and Other Sources

Adero, Malaika, ed. *Up South: Stories, Studies, and Letters of This Century's Black Migrations.* New York: New Press, 1993.

Allen, Theodore W. *The Invention of the White Race: Racial Oppression and Social Control.* London: Verso, 1994.

Atherton, Gertrude. *Senator North.* New York: John Lane, 1900.

Battle, Thomas C., and Clifford Muse. *Howard in Retrospect: Image of the Capstone.* Washington, D.C.: Moorland-Spingarn Research Center, Howard University, 1995.

Benedict, Ruth. *Patterns of Culture.* Boston: Houghton Mifflin, 1934.

Birmingham, Stephen. *Certain People: America's Black Elite.* Boston: Little, Brown and Company, 1977.

Blassingame, John. *Black New Orleans, 1860–1888.* Chicago: University of Chicago Press, 1973.

Boles, John B. *Black Southerners, 1619–1869.* Lexington: University Press of Kentucky, 1983.

Bontemps, Arna. *They Seek a City.* Garden City, N.Y.: Doubleday, 1945.

Boucicault, Dion. *The Octoroon; or, Life in Louisiana.* 1851. Reprint, Miami: Mnemosyne Publishing, 1969.

Brewer, J. Mason. *American Negro Folklore.* Chicago: Quadrangle Books, 1968.

Brooks, Gwendolyn. *The World of Gwendolyn Brooks.* New York: Harper and Row, 1971.

Brown, George Rothwell. *Washington: A Not Too Serious History.* Baltimore: Norman Publishing Company, 1930.

Brown, Sterling. *The Negro in American Fiction.* 1937. Reprint, New York: Arno Press, 1969.

Brown, William Wells. *Clotel, or, The President's Daughter: A Narrative of Slave Life in the United States.* New York: Carol Publishing Group, 1989.

Browne, Ray B. *Popular Beliefs and Practices from Alabama.* Berkeley: Univ. of California Press, 1958.

Bryan, W. Bogart. *A History of the National Capital.* New York: Macmillian, 1914.

Canfield, Dorothy. *The Bent Twig.* New York: Henry Holt, 1915.

Carmichael, Stokley, and Charles Hamilton. *Black Power*. New York: Vintage Books, 1967.

Chapin, F. N. *American Court Gossip, or Life at the National Capitol*. Marshaltown, Iowa: Chapin and Hartwell, 1887.

Child, Lydia Maria. "The Quadroons." Short story published in 1842. Available online at *The Multiracial Activist*, http://www.multiracial.com/readers/child.html.

Clarke, Nina Honemond. *History of the Nineteenth-Century Black Churches in Maryland and Washington, D.C.* Silver Spring, Md.: Bartleby Press, 1983.

Coleman, Chrisena. *Mama Knows Best: African-American Wives' Tales, Myths, and Remedies for Mothers and Mothers-to-Be*. New York: Simon & Schuster, 1997.

Cox, Oliver. *Caste, Class and Race: A Study in Social Dynamics*. Garden City, N.Y.: Doubleday, 1948.

Dance, Daryl Cumber. *From My People: Four Hundred Years of African American Folklore*. New York: Norton, 2002.

———. *Shuckin' and Jivin': Folklore from Contemporary Black Americans*. Bloomington: Indiana University Press, 1978.

Dearborn, Mary V. *Pocahontas's Daughters: Ethnicity and Gender in American Culture*. New York: Oxford University Press, 1986.

A Directory of Churches and Religious Organizations in the District of Columbia. Washington, D.C.: Historical Records Survey, 1939.

Dollard, John. *Caste and Class in a Southern Town*. 1949. Reprint, Garden City, N.Y.: Doubleday, 1957.

Dominguez, Virginia R. *White By Definition: Social Classification in Creole Louisiana*. New Brunswick, N.J.: Rutgers University Press, 1986.

Du Bois, W. E. B. *The Philadelphia Negro: A Social Study*. 1899. Reprinted with a new introduction by Elijah Anderson. Philadelphia: University of Pennsylvania Press, 1996.

Dunbar, Paul Laurence. *Black Literature: Essays*. Columbus, Ohio: Charles E. Merrill Publishing, 1969.

Fauset, Jessie. *The Chinaberry Tree: A Novel of American Life*. 1931. Reprinted with an introduction by Thadious M. Davis. New York: G. K. Hall, 1995.

Fitzpatrick, Sandra, and Maria R. Goodwin. *The Guide to Black Washington: Places and Events of Historical Significance in the Nation's Capital*. New York: Hippocrene Books, 1990.

Ford, Paul Leicester, ed. *The Writings of Thomas Jefferson.* Vol 3. New York: G. P. Putnam's Sons, 1894.

Frazier, Edward Franklin. *Black Bourgeoisie.* Glencoe, Ill.: Free Press, 1957.

Gaines, Ernest J. *Bloodline.* 1968. Reprint, New York: W. W. Norton, 1976.

Gates, Henry Louis, Jr., and Cornel West. *The Future of the Race.* New York: Alfred A. Knopf, 1996.

Gatewood, Willard. *Aristocrats of Color: The Black Elite, 1880–1920.* Bloomington: Indiana University Press, 1990.

Giddings, Paula. *In Search of Sisterhood: Delta Sigma Theta and the Challenge of the Black Sorority Movement.* New York: William Morrow, 1988.

Golden, Marita. *Don't Play in the Sun: One Woman's Journey Through the Color Complex.* New York: Doubleday, 2004.

Graham, Lawrence Otis. *Our Kind of People: Inside America's Black Upper Class.* New York: HarperCollins, 1999.

Green, Constance McLaughlin. *The Secret City: A History of Race Relations in the Nation's Capital.* Princeton, N.J.: Princeton University Press, 1967.

———. *Washington.* 2 vols. Princeton, N.J.: Princeton University Press, 1962–63.

Haizlip, Shirlee Taylor. *The Sweeter the Juice: A Family Memoir in Black and White.* New York: Simon & Schuster, 1994.

Hall, Gwendolyn Midlo. *Social Control in Slave Plantation Societies: A Comparison of St. Dominique and Cuba.* 1971. Reprint, Baton Rouge: Louisiana State University Press, 1996.

Harley, Sharon, and Rosalyn Terborg-Penn, eds. *The Afro-American Woman: Struggles and Images.* Port Washington, N.Y.: Kennikat Press, 1978.

Harper, Frances, E.W. *Iola Leroy, or, Shadows Uplifted.* 1882. Reprinted with a new introduction by Hazel V. Carby. Boston: Beacon Press, 1987.

hooks, bell. *We Real Cool: Black Men and Masculinity.* New York: Routledge, 2004.

Hornsby, Alton, Jr. *Chronology of African American History: Significant Events and People from 1619 to the Present.* Detroit: Gale Research, 1991.

Hudson, Larry, ed. *Working Towards Freedom: Slave Society and Domestic Economy in the American South.* Rochester, N.Y.: University of Rochester Press, 1994.

Hughes, Langston. "Passing." Chapter 4 in *The Ways of White Folks.* New York: Alfred A. Knopf, 1934.

———, ed. *The Book of Negro Humor.* New York: Dodd, Mead, 1966.

Hurston, Zora Neale. *Dust Tracks on a Road: An Autobiography.* 1942. Reprint, New York: HarperCollins, 1995.

Ingraham, Joseph Holt. *The Quadroone; or St. Michael's Day.* 1841. Reprint, Kessinger Publishing, 2004.

Johnson, Allan. *Surviving Freedom: The Black Community of Washington, D.C., 1860–1880.* New York: Garland, 1993.

Johnson, Georgia Douglas. "Blue Blood." In *Fifty More Contemporary One-Act Plays,* edited by Frank Shay. New York: D. Appleton and Company, 1928.

Johnson, Georgia Douglas Camp. *Bronze: A Book of Verse.* 1922. Reprinted with an Introduction by W. E. B. Du Bois. Freeport: Books for Libraries Press, 1971.

Johnson, Haynes. *Dusk at the Mountain: The Negro, the Nation, and the Capital; A Report on Problems and Progress.* Garden City: Doubleday, 1963.

Johnston, James Hugo. *Miscegenation in the Ante-bellum South.* Chicago: University of Chicago Libraries, 1939.

Jones, William Henry. *The Housing of Negroes in Washington, D.C.: A Study in Human Ecology.* Washington, D.C.: Howard University Press, 1929.

———. *Recreation and Amusement Among Negroes in Washington, D.C.: A Sociological Analysis of the Negro in an Urban Environment.* 1927. Reprint, Westport, Conn.: Negro Universities Press, 1970.

Katz, Bernard, ed. *The Social Implications of Early Negro Music in the United States; with Over 150 of the Songs, Many of Them with Their Music.* New York: Arno Press, 1969.

Keckley, Elizabeth. *Behind the Scenes.* New York: G. W. Carleton, 1868.

Keil, Charles. *Urban Blues.* Chicago: University of Chicago Press, 1966.

Kennedy, Randall. *Nigger: The Strange Career of a Troublesome Word.* New York: Pantheon Books, 2002.

Keyes, Frances Parkinson. *Crescent Carnival.* New York: Franklin Watts, 1942.

Koger, Larry. *Black Slaveowners: Free Black Slave Masters in South Carolina, 1790–1860.* Jefferson, N.C.: MacFarland, 1985.

Krehbiel, Edward Henry. *A Study of Racial National Music, Afro-American Folk Songs.* 1914. Reprint, New York: Frederick Ungar, 1971.

Larsen, Nella. *Quicksand* and *Passing.* Edited by Deborah E. McDowell. American Women Writers Series. New Brunswick, N.J.: Rutgers University Press, 1986.

Larson, Charles. *Invisible Darkness: Jean Toomer and Nella Larsen.* Iowa City: University of Iowa Press, 1993.

Lee, Reba. *I Passed for White.* As told to Mary Hastings Bradley. New York: Longmans, Green, 1955.

Lessoff, Alan. *The Nation and Its City: Politics, "Corruption," and Progress in Washington, D.C.* Baltimore: Johns Hopkins University Press, 1994.

Loewenberg, Bert James, and Ruth Bogin, eds. *Black Women in Nineteenth Century American Life: Their Words, Their Thoughts, Their Feelings.* University Park: Pennsylvania State University Press, 1976.

Logan, Frenise Avedis. *The Negro in North Carolina, 1876–1894.* Chapel Hill: University of North Carolina Press, 1964.

Logan, Rayford W. *Howard University: The First Hundred Years, 1867–1967.* New York: New York University Press, 1969.

Mathabane, Mark. *Kaffir Boy in America: An Encounter with Apartheid.* New York: Charles Scribner's Sons, 1989.

McKay, Claude. *Complete Poems.* Edited and with an introduction by William J. Maxwell. Urbana: University of Illinois Press, 2004.

———. *A Long Way from Home.* 1937. Reprint, New York: Arno Press, 1969.

Mencke, John G. *Mulattoes and Race Mixture: American Attitudes and Images, 1865–1918.* Ann Arbor, Mich.: UMI Research Press, 1979.

Miller, Arthur G., ed. *In the Eye of the Beholder: Contemporary Issues in Stereotyping.* New York: Praeger, 1982.

Mitchell, Mary. *Chronicles of Georgetown Life, 1865–1900.* Cabin John, Md.: Seven Locks Press, 1986.

Moss, Alfred A., Jr. *The American Negro Academy: Voice of the Talented Tenth.* 1977. Reprint, Baton Rouge: Louisiana State University Press, 1981.

Myrdal, Gunnar. *An American Dilemma: The Negro Problem and Modern Democracy.* Vol. 2. New York: Harper and Brothers, 1944.

Neverdon-Morton, Cynthia. *Afro-American Women of the South and the Advancement of the Race, 1895–1925.* Knoxville: University of Tennessee Press, 1989.

O'Daniel, Therman B. *Jean Toomer: A Critical Evaluation.* Washington, D.C.: Howard University Press, 1988.

Odum, Howard W., and Guy B. Johnson. *The Negro and His Songs: A Study of Typical Negro Songs in the South.* Chapel Hill: University of North Carolina Press, 1925.

Oliver, Paul. *Blues Fell This Morning: Meaning in the Blues.* 2nd ed. Cambridge: Cambridge University Press, 1990.

Ottley, Roi, and William J. Weatherby, eds. *The Negro in New York: An Informal Social History, 1626–1940.* New York: New York Public Library, 1967.

Perkins, A. E., ed. *Who's Who in Colored Louisiana.* Baton Rouge, La.: Douglas Loan, 1939.

Peterkin, Julia. *Bright Skin.* Indianapolis: Bobbs-Merrill, 1932

Peacocke, James S. *The Creole Orphans; or Lights and Shadows of Southern Life; A Tale of Louisiana.* New York: Derby and Jackson, 1856.

Picquet, Louisa. *The Octoroon: A Tale of Southern Slave Life.* 1861. Reprinted in *Collected Black Women's Narratives.* Schomburg Library of Nineteenth-Century Black Women Writers. Edited by Henry Louis Gates Jr. New York: Oxford University Press, 1988.

Prahlad, Sw. Anand. *African American Proverbs in Context.* Jackson: University Press of Mississippi, 1996.

Rabinowitz, Howard N. *Race Relations in the Urban South, 1865–1890.* New York: Oxford University Press, 1978.

Ralph, Julian. *Dixie; or, Southern Scenes and Sketches.* New York: Harper and Brothers, 1896.

Reuter, Edward Byron. *The Mulatto in the United States, Including a Study of the Role of Mixed-Blood Races Throughout the World.* 1918. Reprint, New York: Negro Universities Press, 1969.

Reid, Captain Mayne. *The Quadroon; or, A Lover's Adventures in Louisiana.* New York: Robert M. DeWitt, 1856.

Rooks, Noliwe M. *Hair Raising: Beauty, Culture, and African American Women.* New Brunswick, N.J.: Rutgers University Press, 1996.

Russell, Kathy, Midge Wilson, and Ronald Hall. *The Color Complex: The Politics of Color among African Americans.* New York: Harcourt Brace Jovanovich, 1992.

Scales-Trent, Judy. *Notes of a White Black Woman: Race, Color, and Community.* University Park: Pennsylvania State University Press, 1995.

Schuyler, George. *Black No More: A Novel.* 1931. Reprint, New York: Modern Library, 1999.

Shakur, Assata. *Assata: An Autobiography.* Westport, CT: Lawrence Hill, 1987.

Shange, Ntozake. *for colored girls who have considered suicide / when the rainbow is enuf.* New York: Macmillan, 1977.

Shannon, A. H. *The Negro in Washington: A Study in Race Amalgamation.* New York: W. Neale, 1930.

Smythwick, Charles A., Jr. *False Measure: A Satirical Novel of the Lives and Objectives of Upper Middle-Class Negroes.* New York: William-Frederick Press, 1954.

Snethen, Worthington G. *The Black Code of the District of Columbia, in Force September 1st.* New York: A. & F. Anti-Slavery Society, 1848.

Sollors, Werner. *Neither Black nor White yet Both: Thematic Explorations of Interracial Literature.* 1997. Reprint, Cambridge, Mass: Harvard University Press, 1999.

Somerville, Siobhan B. *Queering the Color Line: Race and the Invention of Homo-sexuality in American Culture.* Durham, N.C.: Duke University Press, 2000.

Spalding, Henry D., ed. *Encyclopedia of Black Folklore and Humor.* Middle Village, N.Y.: Jonathan David Publishers, 1972.

Steen, Marguerite. *The Sun Is My Undoing.* New York: Viking Press, 1941.

Stribling, T. S. *Birthright.* New York: Century, 1922.

Taft, Michael, ed. *Blues Lyric Poetry: An Anthology.* New York: Garland Press, 1983.

Terrell, Mary Church. *A Colored Woman in a White World.* 1940. Reprint, New York: G. K. Hall & Co., 1996.

Thompson, Dolphin G. *A Picture Guide to Black America in Washington, D.C.* Washington, D.C.: Brownson House, 1976.

Thurman, Wallace. *The Blacker the Berry: A Novel of Negro Life.* 1929. Reprinted with an introduction by Therman B. O'Daniel. New York: Collier Books, 1970.

Van Notten, Eleonore. *Wallace Thurman's Harlem Renaissance.* Atlanta: Rodopi, 1994.

Wallace, Michele. *Black Macho and the Myth of the Superwoman.* 1979. Reprinted with new introduction and bibliography. London: Verso Press, 1990.

Washington, Booker T. *Up From Slavery.* 1901. Reprint, New York: Signet Classics, 1969.

Washington, Booker T., N. B. Wood, and Fannie Barrier Williams. *A New Negro for a New Century.* Chicago: American Publishing House, 1900.

Whyte, James Huntington. *The Uncivil War: Washington During the Reconstruction.* New York: Twayne Publishers, 1958

Williams, Gregory Howard. *Life on the Color Line: The True Story of a White Boy Who Discovered He Was Black.* New York: Dutton, 1995.

Wish, Harvey, ed. *Slavery in the South: First-Hand Accounts of the Antebellum American Southland from Northern and Southern Whites, Negroes, and Foreign Observers.* New York: Farrar, Straus, 1964.

Wolfe, George C. *The Colored Museum.* 1988. New York: Broadway Play Publishers, 1988.

Zack, Naomi. *Race and Mixed Race.* Philadelphia: Temple University Press, 1993.

Zumwalt, Rosemary. *American Folklore Scholarship: A Dialogue of Dissent.* Bloom-ington: Indiana University Press, 1988.

Index

The Paper Bag Principle was designed and typeset on a Macintosh computer system using QuarkXPress software. The body text is set in 10/14 Minion and display type is set in Prestige. This book was designed and typeset by Kelly Gray.